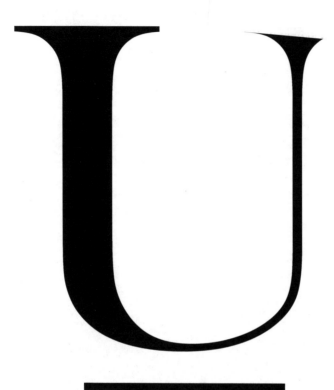

UNDERSCORE

UEA UNDERGRADUATE
CREATIVE WRITING ANTHOLOGY

2020

U

NOTE FROM THE EDITORS

This marks the seventh year that UEA has produced an anthology that highlights the cream of the crop from their undergraduate creative writing students. It is also the fourth year that we, Egg Box, have had the honour of producing the book you now see before you and will be, due to recent developments, the first ever Egg Box eBook. When we first drafted this note just a few short months ago, none of us could ever have expected such a change in circumstances as the one we find ourselves in now the world over. Although this book contains works and was worked on by UEA students, they hail from all corners of the globe and so it is a testament to their passion for the subject that they continued tirelessly to help produce this anthology even whilst arranging travel home or feeling the pressure of social distancing. So we begin with a whole hearted thanks to them and wish them well.

Egg Box are both a society and the student led press at UEA, encouraging students in all areas that come under the banner of publishing. Be it the creative side, designing, or project management, Egg Box has always welcomed students from all faculties and helped them develop a greater understanding of the publishing process. The Undergraduate Creative Writing Anthology would not be possible without the diligent efforts of student volunteers who have offered up their time to help us whittle down over a hundred submissions to the fifty-five here for you to read. If you turn to the back of this book you will see the names of those who worked diligently for this anthology to happen, including the Egg Box committee who have not only helped shape this project but also produced countless workshops and creative opportunities for our members that truly make our society a community.

The UEA Undergraduate Creative Writing Anthology is a truly unique collection that never ceases to disappoint year by year. The talent that UEA inspires is no wonder when you consider its location. Norwich is the first UNESCO City of Literature and a place that for hundreds of years has been a key player in the shaping of creative thought. On any given evening poetry readings and open mics are performed, new plays are premiered and across the city hundreds of people come together to appreciate the power of words.

Here is just a taste of the talent this wonderful city and university inspires, it would not have been possible without the support of Nathan Hamilton and Philip Langeskov, alongside funding and encouragement from the school of Literature, Drama and Creative Writing. The editorial team hope you enjoy reading this anthology as much as we enjoyed making it. To see a project grow from an initial meeting about titles, to seeing the final cover design, to reading it on our screens and, hopefully one day soon, to hold the book in our hands was a truly incredible experience and one that we hope you can feel the passion for on every page.

Enjoy and be well,

The Editorial Team

Contents —

10	**Shell**	Jordan Aitcheson
11	**California Dreamin'**	Joe Bird
14	**We Shoplift Glitter on Friday 13th**	Thai Braddick
16	**Echo**	Leia Butler
17	**Word ladder**	Leia Butler
18	**Cast**	Daisy Campbell
20	**Carved Without a Smile**	Charlotte Cassidy
24	**Pride And Prophecy,**	Andrew Constantinou
28	**On falling in love with your childhood best friend.**	Dylan Davies
29	**On being the first to move on.**	Dylan Davies
31	**STAEDTLER® Mars Plastic**	Sasha Donovan-Anns
35	**Choke**	Helen Drumm
39	**It was after my first death**	Isabel Edain
41	**Incarnate**	Ally Fowler

40	**Grater** Chloe Gainford
48	**Seventy Million Tills** Sebastian Gale
49	**Notes to a younger self…** Emma Goodyear
50	**Longing** Emma Goodyear
51	**My Illness Has Teeth** Samuel Gordon Webb
54	**Your Two Minutes Hate** Alex Grenfell 51
56	**In your grandparents' living room, aged seven** Oliver Hancock 53
57	**Conscience** Oliver Hancock
58	**An anonymous Space TripAdvisor® review of 'Planet Earth'** Ida Hansen
59	**Keeping Company** Kasper Hassett
62	**Yours Alone** Maddi Hastings
63	**THE EGG** Siobhan Horner-Galvin
70	**Rollicking Randy Dandy Oh.** Charlie Humphreys
74	**Photobook** Ben'J Jordan

75	**Hugo Simberg, The Garden of Death, 1896** Erin Ketteridge
79	**Vows** Erin Ketteridge
81	**Salt Flats** Sebastian Lloyd
82	**There, There** Chris Matthews
83	**Tuna and Mangoes** Zoe Mitchell
87	**A Certain Cartesian Anxiety** Arcadia Molinas-Argimon
88	**112** Arcadia Molinas-Argimon
89	**Sterilisation** Farah Mostafa
90	**Safe** Farah Mostafa
91	**Milk Dregs** Farah Mostafa
92	**Flash Fictions I** Chiara Picchi
93	**Flash Fictions II** Chiara Picchi
94	**Abych koupil rybu*** Jack Pletts
98	**Momentary** Jeanie Purslow
100	**27 Cheap Things To Help Solve Life's Annoying Little Problems** Rose Ramsden

101	**Teeth**	
	Rose Ramsden	
102	**The Wheelbarrow Cross**	
	Cormac Rea	
106	**Plath's First Cut**	
	Julia Reynolds	
107	**Baby Got Basiphobia**	
	Saskia Reynolds	
112	**Latte with Soya**	
	Tom Rosser	
115	**Decade Number Two**	
	Leo Schrey-Yeats	
119	**Before the First Date: You**	
	Oliver Shrouder	
121	**The Ages of Memory**	
	Toby Skinner	
123	**Ladybirds**	
	Lily Stirling	
126	**When the weatherman sleeps**	
	Madu Udeh	
128	**Starlight**	
	Megan Watts	
129	**Faces of Grief**	
	Shi Yap	
132	**Cleansing Shallows**	
	Katherine Yong Yhap	

Shell
Jordan Aitcheson

"The bird struggles out of the egg. The egg is the world. Whoever wants to be born, must first destroy a world." Herman Hesse, Demain

I pray I get out of Eden Park.
I've got love for the sacrifices that got me there.
My parents bent back and bone,
and argued and fought, to attain
the normality of the life
that they sought;
yet I cannot
stay forever.

The shell we are raised in
isn't to be replicated
in unfathomable precision.
It isn't all good,
nothing is.
We should recognise,
when we start to act as fully
fleshed extensions
of what is immediately around us.

You must get out.
There is an undeniable eagerness
in us all to break the
cycle once we recognise it.
So, I pray I get out of Eden Park.
I pray I break my shell.

California Dreamin'
Joe Bird

1967.
Way in front of the Pontiac's hood the tarmac of the boulevard shimmers and melts under the pressing heat and excitement of California. A circle of tin can Hobos at the end of Route 15 that inspired a generation of kids to flip off the country and their parents, and to bomb it three sheets to the wind down the freeway until they could smell the marijuana. Streets upon bustling streets of acidic smiles and tobacco-stained teeth, the sweet tantalising promise of the world in your hands, burgers and short shorts that don't quite fit. Hairy, black-toothed rednecks and shining, suited Yanks, movie stars and models, the re-ignited embers of the American Dream, burning bright enough to compete with the beating sun. I watch the road carry us West towards Brentwood, a sweating, gray, conveyor-belt punctuated with palms, sweet golden girls in the prime of their innocent and promising youth, bedraggled Berkley-type bohemians smoking tea in groups of purposely frayed and stained rags, countless shouting billboards and signs looking to drain my wallet for liquor, girls, Coca-Cola, food...

"Pass us that bag?"

The dense air tickles the hair on my arm resting out the window of the backseat, drying the steady stream of sweat that futilely battles the warmth of the cross-hatched asphalt streets of the West. Taking the final drag of my cigarette, I flick it to the sizzling curb and slide another out of the packet in the breast pocket of my shirt. On the corner of South Mansfield Avenue, a line of police Diplomats are all parked in a row in the parking lot of L.A. Burger, their tubby drivers milling around the turquoise square building, dabbing the sweat that steadily streams from beneath their caps and shoving burgers wrapped in yellow napkins into their dripping mouths.

"Kid..."

What a journey that awaits me. First Sacramento, then Salt Lake City for kicks with Max, and then the world's mine oyster, which I with sword will open! The car soars over the tarmac, slipping between bright, varnished bumpers. Flying through each intersection, I catch winks from the Griffith Observatory, casting its wise old cosmic eye over the crowded debauchery of modern-day Los Angeles, silently frowning its telescopic brow at the sex, rebellion and downright recklessness of the 21st Century– If only they could see us now!

"Kid... Pass me that bag in the back!"

My cigarette falls out of my hand onto the road.

"Sorry." I fumble the surprisingly heavy duffle bag over to the meaty, ringed fingers that await it, belonging to the guy in the passenger seat.

"Long gone for a moment there, ay kid." Says the driver, through clouds of smoke. I know neither of their names, but these guys definitely have had the nicest motor since my journey back from the border. I smile and mumble apologetically again, taking another cigarette. These men have lungs like steam trains and the intimidating demeanour of alcoholic silverbacks so in the name of good will I better follow suit. With a scant purple fur coat hanging off her shoulders, a fish-netted woman pulls a drooling dog by his tie through the curtained door of a dilapidated 'THEATRE'. A preacher shuffles his feet deeper into the dirt, ash and grime of the sidewalk with each prophetic word mumbled from his quivering lips. Now is not the time to be a God-fearing old man. In a city of sinful passions and pleasures one will do best to gratify all of his as immediately as possible before our short fuses fizzle out. The driver turns to me as we slow at the intersection for South Crescent Heights.

"We're gonna have to make a quick stop in a second but whilst we're there you can climb into the front and keep her ticking for us."

I don't question why, as we turn left at the intersection and follow the road a couple hundred feet, rolling to a stop beside a big white cinema billboard spelling 'IN COLD BLOOD' in thick black letters.

"Here we go. Keep her on and jump in front kid." Says Meathands, grabbing the bag in the footwell by his feet.

Out on the street they mill around the boot of the car for a second then walks towards the entrance. Climbing over into the driver's seat, just before they walk underneath the shade of the billboard, I see a flash of silver in the waistband of Meathands' jeans, before he flicks his Birds of Paradise shirt over his belt and walks into the foyer.

My stomach drops and sweat drips off my brow on to my chest. Breathless, my hands dance over the polished steering wheel. Adrenaline balls up in my stomach and shoots across my body, vibrating my hands and tensing my legs, rooting my heels in the footwell under the pedals. The Mama's and Papa's dream their radio dreams of California, cutting through the dread that now streams out of the windows of the car in great plumes, above the cinema and up towards the burning sun.

***

Time passes outside the cinema, six-point-five litres of growling American muscle vibrating beneath my feet. In a delirious fog, I grab the handbrake of the car and push it down, freeing the four wheels on the flat road. Hands on the wheel. Constantly looking over my shoulder towards the caramelized glass doors of the cinema, I'm expecting them to catch me. Before I can put the clutch down, I curse my ability to overthink and pull the brake up – they did not look afraid to use them, presuming they both had one. God knows what else men like Meathands & Co wouldn't be afraid to do.

Outside the car, two muted bangs permeate the film of my anxiety. Snapping my neck round in nervous anticipation, I see the reflection of the street split in two and give way to the two men sprinting towards the vehicle.

"Let's go kid, let's go!" Says the driver, who's spindly shoulders look so sharp before they give way to his long reedy arms. Like a Mantis.

I slam the clutch down and gun the fucker, as they bowl themselves into the backseat.Back on the Boulevard. The colours have changed. Riding the highs of adrenaline, the bright sun and fluorescent colours blind me as the humid air whips my face, drying my eyeballs red as we cut through traffic, weaving between more glaring chrome bumpers—a shining, mechanic eel of chaos snaking through this clammy, Californian river of asphalt.

"Mother- fucking—A man!!" I clock Mantis in the rear-view pouring money out of the duffle bag, onto his lap.

Meathands is grinning, sifting through the notes spilled on the backseat with a green gleam of delight across his face. He leans over the front seat, grabbing a black leather purse from the glovebox. Out of the purse he pulls a small glass vial, that he upturns onto the tendon between his thumb and forefinger, spilling flaky white powder all over his lap as the wheels of the Pontiac try their best to ignore the potholes.

"Watch it with that! We're still in broad fucking daylight." Mantis warns, snatching the black purse as Meathands loudly snorts the powder into his nose, before licking the surface of his hand clean.

"What are you worried about? We've got the money and the kid's doing good!" he says nasally, winking at me through the rear-view mirror as we continue snaking down the boulevard. "Success so far kid – want some?"

Mantis interjects before I can reply, "You don't have to do anything kid just get us to Canoga Park, we can't piss this opportunity away getting pulled because of you."

"Give him a chance to speak for himself…" Meathands wiggles the vial beside my ear, grinning through the rear view.

"I'm good. Thanks."

Every few seconds I think I see a flash of blue behind me, plunging me into sweaty fits of anxiety. My hands slip on the varnished wood of the steering wheel, swerving the car way too close to the rear of a rusted, brown Falcon packed up with the lives and memories of a migrating family of four – the corrupted depravity of the botoxed, rehabbed land of palms and promise too much for them, teeth-gritted and white knuckled as they race out of the city. I should know. What the fuck is happening?

Shakily I slide a cigarette out of my breast and into my mouth. Meathands pokes a lighter in front of me and leaning into it, I see a blink of blue pass between cars a few hundred feet back. Pulling the flame into the head of tobacco, thin wisps of smoke escape my mouth and flower in front of me as I see it again, moving up the lanes of traffic, reeling itself towards me like a fish on a line. It's unmistakable, a great shining, flashing white tooth of authority pushing through the traffic. Shit. I'm sandwiched between two Fords and can only watch as vehicles give way to the screeching wail of urgency that rides up the far lane, closer by the second. They've both noticed it too, turning their heads back in fear as we cruise the current of the traffic, unable to escape or hide. My heart is thumping in my ears and my stomach drops, somersaulting onto the pedals in the footwell below. Maybe I can get out of this, absolve myself of responsibility—I didn't have a clue this was going to happen. Should have bailed when I had the chance. Some aged and ludicrous sense of adolescent hunger, a lust for danger and irresponsibility, was keeping me in front of that steering wheel. How would that save my ass when I go down for driving the getaway car. Three cars behind now and we still can't budge. The fish has swallowed the worm. I take a big drag of my cigarette, satisfyingly charring my lungs and burning my throat as I exhale, and crane my neck out the window to watch the Diplomat dart past, shooting down the boulevard to some unknown producers out-of-control cocaine fuelled sex party, or who knows.

A space to my right appears and without needing to be told twice, I swerve at the intersection, off the boulevard and onto a relatively quiet side street, pulling the car over and slamming my back into the seat, my hands still tightly gripping the wheel.

We Shoplift Glitter on Friday 13th
Thai Braddick

No table, no chairs, you're on the floor
sprawled with your friend staring sullen
at the ceiling light. December has been
twelve years too long and you're afraid
of the world turning twenty. Hands shaking
into hands, Friday 13th and your fingernails
are painted with shoplifted glitter, and chipping
like old terrace bricks. You roll over,
a pearl escaping the oyster's jaw, sighing,
and you say "I'm so tired, how do I go on?
Don't have my meds, fighting a fight all lost."
Your friend kisses your head, and it hurts
their fractured rib, and you say "Are you okay?"
"My shitty rib means I have more room
in my heart for you. Let's get your meds."
Rib cracked whilst they fought, like you
with your cracked skull, cracked heart,
you stand up together and hug and it hurts
but it reminds you hope isn't lost and you
stumble, broken bones and frostbitten flesh
towards an empty flat, no electricity
with shoplifted bread you stole just to eat something.
You say, "It's so cold in my flat, can I stay with you?"
And all curly haired and handsome your friend says,
"I'll help you pack." You almost cry.
This is what a community looks like, you think,
all broken and putting socks, toothbrush,
butter, into plastic bags. The bus arrives
on time (for once) and you get in together,
cracked head on broken shoulder, jaws clenched,
you stop by the corner shop (five minutes
more to walk) and you have forty pounds.
You spend thirty pounds on food, so you can survive,
you spend ten pounds on half-dead flowers
so you can live. And you go back to the house
sad but hardened, sad but hopeful, sad but
the house opens up warm and you sit back against
the wall and hold each other. You take your meds,
free and crucial and necessary and
you feel yourself becoming yourself again.
You light a candle in the dark, and suddenly
you're alive again. Suddenly, no tables, no chairs

and the floor is the foundation you build up from again.
The flowers bloom only slightly in fresh, cold
December water.

Echo
Leia Butler

focus on me
    dark room, dilated eyes
                                      give me the raise
                                        take in my gaze

don't be telling me that you're steaming and you feel like screaming
                and she's not replying
    bc I'm here holding your hand, keeping you afloat
and I'm raging   and it's all I can do not to rock the boat
    and I'm screaming
and I bite my lip for blood   and my heart is pounding

                                  call it love on a
and my head is spinning
        bc you're telling me you feel alone
and you can't stop staring at your fucking phone

        don't worry hun,
            let the wave pass
        I'll be her for a bit

                            I'm not bad at heart
                                just think you need to restart
                                    lose each other
                                      find a different
    I'll look up at a sky of disarray
until I go fucking crazy

    but it's alright babe,
I'll play the long game

Word Ladder
Leia Butler

Down — town and — torn but — turn, — burn. Re — born. Now — rise, — ride the — tide. — Time? Its — mine to — mind.

~~Go down the~~ ~~word ladder,~~ ~~squared and~~ ~~ensnared.~~

Fall — fail and — wail. But — sail, find — soil. A new — soul now. — Rise, you're — ripe, it's a — rite. A free — kite, day & — nite — End, on a good — note.

Cast
Daisy Campbell

Kneading harlequin sardines,
I'll watch virgin paint born writhing.

My muslin-draped windows screen
a spiteful sky.
Starkly. Skulking to flinch and inflict
impatient fits of
gold slashed on bruises,
brooding.
They subdue the silently established
solitary
parade of growls,
successive and close,
pacing, paced by a lag in sound
which courts the violent glint
of a facet of a ring
in the firmament.
I always get a headache in this weather.
Bet she's cold.
Altruistically, I'll light
a candle to warm her skin
tones.

Surrounded by scraps,
I perform forgeries of alchemy
for those wanting resurrection.
It won't happen, but I'll give you
an eternal feigned skin—
will varnish you in
a wall where leaves are irises' flecks,
apples are your lips,
the crisp edge of linen
is the glint in your eye.
Never use black. Not for your jet,
not for your pupils:
hues. Apparently,
nothing is that dark,
externally.
Gesso. Tempera.
And I've slaughtered
a bird for translucence.
Stillborn, unborn, but
still.

Snags—in my throat—a tainted water.
Noxious blood-thinning bane
to the pallor I embalm on canvas.
I'll gift the glass a muddy eddy,
of excess.
Deposit.

Counterfeit stifled breath in daubing.
Stipple a complexion, mapped.
Lesioned lips of palpable impasto.
Forcing eyes ablaze with colours
bleeding.
Focus. Her peripheral
rendered a sweet vignette.
As rasping bristles coax a fever,
I swatch a desiccated rose
for her bone's shroud.

I'll borrow beetle backs for now,
bequeathing florid stains
of sanguine warmth.
Red.
Blood.
A deep shellac.

Carved Without a Smile
Charlotte Cassidy

"You ever wonder why you never see a statue with a smile?" I asked as I took my plate to the sink and looked out of the window. There were four statues outside, all sculpted as naked Greek goddesses. They were at the back of the garden, each stood on a corner of the four stone walls. Inside the stone walls was a square flowerbed, but there were no plants. The Landlord said that he had salted the soil as the red pansies were distracting. He had also said that he trusted us to protect the statues, despite us all being boys in our second year of university.

"Statues aren't supposed to smile, Hayden," Zeus said before sipping his beer, "No one was happy in the past."

Term had begun over a week ago. I still wasn't used to living away from student accommodation. I now rented a five-bedroom house with thin walls and single-glazed windows that let a chilly draft through the panes. Mould was beginning to ruin the ceilings. But, it was still home, even though I only knew one of my housemates: Zeus. He was the president of both Warwick's History Society and the swimming team, with curly blonde hair and a Greek nose, whilst I was a skinny philosophy student who had his tongue pierced. We first spoke when I needed help unlocking my room. On our first night out, he was my wingman energised on vodka and coke. He charmed a redhead into kissing me.

Her name was Zoe and she became my girlfriend the following week. Zoe was my very own Scouse statue. I stick-and-poked my initials on her middle finger for our one-month anniversary and she cut my hair monthly with kitchen scissors. We spent days in a kaleidoscope, debating our philosophies. Zoe joked that Zeus was Warwick University's very own god, seeing as girls would get on their knees just for his acknowledgement.

Then Zeus said that Zoe had kissed him at his birthday party in April. I had never cried in front of him before. He took me on a bar crawl and brought me drinks until I blacked out. The next morning, he said that I had broken up with Zoe over the phone in a series of drunken yells. She texted me paragraphs but I refused to read them. When I moved into the new house, all of my memories with Zoe became buried.

"I think we should have a party. On Friday." Zeus decided a couple minutes later as I was drying a spoon with a heavily stained tea-towel. "One for the History Society. All of the freshers were awkward, one of them called me 'sir'. But that won't last for long if I get them absolutely pissed. Especially Sheepskin-Girl."

"'Sheepskin-Girl'?" I asked.

"This Fresher that was there. I've forgotten her name but not the sheepskin jacket she was wearing. We got on really well. I mean, she called me a twat but—"

"A twat?"

"Well, she called my parents twats for naming me 'Zeus'."

"And you want this girl to come to this party because…?"

"She's interesting. She's like a song I can't get out of my head. I mean, the lyrics are a bit shit, but it has a catchy beat."

I hesitated, feeling the draft from the window on my neck. "You think the statues will survive a party?"

"We'll keep the garden off limits. Besides, it's second year; it's time to start living like Gods." We decorated our house in several sets of fairy lights, making every room glow golden. The freshers arrived at ten and clung to one side of the room, with their bottles of wine or Lambrini. Fortunately, Zeus brought down his deck of cards and taught them how to play Ring of Fire. By the end of the first round, all of the first-years' bottles were empty so Zeus gave them a shot of tequila each. One of the girls nearly threw up on me afterwards. I was sitting on the beer-stained sofa and speaking to a housemate about how annoying the Landlord was for turning up – unannounced – with gardening tools that morning.

The party continued into the next day through drunk conversations. There had been a debate about Brexit and someone had ordered a pizza but a Fresher spilled their white wine on it, seconds after delivery. I was discussing philosophy with someone from the swimming team who faintly smelt of chlorine. I always found the world an easier place to understand when my intoxicated head was spinning with it. Gold Digger was playing quietly in the background whilst I was explaining the concept of determinism.

"The human experience is just a chain of reactions," I said. "And that's why it's hard to pinpoint who is responsible for what."

There was a thud on the sofa, making me spill some of my vodka lemonade on my neck and it trickled down my shirt. As my fingers became sticky from rubbing my collarbone, I turned to face a girl with curly brunette hair. She smelt of seduction wrapped up in rose petals and looked like an experienced heartbreaker.

I realised who she was, after seeing her sheepskin jacket.

"That whole 'everyone is responsible' idea is bullshit," Sheepskin-Girl said abrasively in a Mancunian accent. She had red wine stained around her mouth.

I straightened my shoulders. "No action is purely someone's own."

"What if someone murdered a kid? It would be obvious who to punish."

"What if they had been drugged so they weren't acting rationally?"

"They're still a murderer."

"It's not as simple as that."

"It's easy to go through life without fucking murdering anyone."

Before I could answer, Zeus sat on the sofa's leather arm and began stroking the wool-collar of Sheepskin-Girl's sheepskin jacket as he teased her. I sank back into the pillows and looked up at the growing splodge of mould in the back-left corner of the ceiling; I wondered if the landlord knew. Zeus told Sheepskin-Girl about how he'd fractured his ankle whilst skiing in Austria a couple months ago. She called him a 'posh Tory'. Across the room, on the coral armchair, there was a man with a girl straddling him as they made out. His hands had disappeared up her shirt. Her hair was coloured turquoise.

I thought of Zoe.

I remembered how I let her dye my blue hair back to its natural hazelnut colour. I feared university being a repetition of sixth-form, where it was difficult to find myself in school photos, yet I didn't need bright colours once life was no longer bleak. She got frustrated when her hair kept on getting in the way of her face, but the dye-covered gloves restricted her to whipping her head back every twenty seconds. She almost stormed out when I called her an idiot for not tying up her hair beforehand.

I knew I loved her when she brought me a new towel the following day. There were times when I wished the two of us could return to that small bathroom—she could cut my hair, and I would laugh at her when she cursed. But another Fresher now lived in that little en suite.

"Hayden, watch her. I'm just going to get her another drink, yeah?" Zeus said as he got up and left the room.

An hour had gone by, and I was slumped so far down the sofa that my legs were hanging off. I sat up, my neck ached and the taste of vodka was bitterly stale in my mouth. Several people were sleeping on the floor and a bottle of red wine had spilled over. Luckily, we didn't have carpets.

"He keeps on giving me drinks." Sheepskin-Girl sat up with difficulty, hand pressed against her forehead. "I wasn't supposed to get this drunk."

I didn't reply and instead listened to Blurred Lines playing on the speaker.

"You look pissed off," Sheepskin-Girl said.

I glared at her and inhaled heavily.

Sheepskin-Girl stayed silent as she fell back into the sofa. "I think God forgot to install a mute button in me. I wasn't supposed to still be like this when I went to university... people don't want to be friends with a bitch," she said.

Sighing, I ran a hand through my hair. "You're not a bitch."

"Hayden," Sheepskin-Girl grabbed the middle of my shirt, which was still damp from vodka lemonade, and pulled herself up, "you won't let anything happen to me, right?"

"What do you mean?"

"Stay with me for the rest of the night, okay?"

"Zeus will look after you."

"No. You need to take care of me."

"He's a good guy."

"Zeus is too drunk and he likes me. It's a bad idea—everything is a bad idea—I'm too drunk. I need to get home."

"You won't get home safely, trust me. You need fresh air." I helped her up. She collapsed against my chest as I pulled her arm over my shoulders and we stepped into the garden. The porch light turned on whilst I helped her over to the statues. She sat on the stone wall and fell back onto the soil. Her legs were spread out and her skirt was raised over her waist. I saw that she had a doe tattooed on her thigh before the light switched off. I cursed before rushing inside.

Zeus was in the kitchen, hugging a Fresher who was sobbing about his ex. I got a glass out of the cupboard.

"God, women can be evil." Zeus stumbled over to me.

"Your girl's in the garden, she needs water," I said before turning the tap off.

"Don't worry mate, I'll give it to her." Zeus grabbed the glass out of my hand. "Start kicking people out, yeah?"

I went to the living room and turned the speaker off. People began collecting their half-emptied bottles and coats that were stuffed behind the sofas or hanging off doors. There was still a girl asleep on the floor a few minutes later, her fingertips dipped in the red puddle of wine. I shook her shoulder, making her moan and slowly stand. I got up and looked out of the window. I couldn't see anything outside, only the living room reflected back at me.

Pulling the back-door handle, I stepped outside. There was a low grunting noise, like a man punishing the darkness. The porch light switched on. Zeus' trousers were around his ankles and he was thrusting into the girl lying limp against the flowerbed.

In the night, I saw a monster.

I rushed back inside. Zeus was my friend. He cooked me fry-ups when I was hungover, he had introduced me to most of the people that had become my closest friends, he was the reason I met Zoe.

Zoe.

Collapsing on the sofa in the now empty living room, I grabbed my phone and found Zoe's unread texts. Four letters.

Rape.

My phone dropped from my hands as the backdoor opened. I looked up to see Zeus. A red thong was hanging out of his pocket.

"She's okay. Just pretty fucked," Zeus said breathlessly before leaving the room.

Turning to my left, I saw Sheepskin-Girl's jacket. I picked it up and smelt that dangerously seductive scent.

"Is that Carmen's?" the girl, who was unconscious moments ago, asked as she gestured to the jacket. "Is she okay?"

"Sh-she's in… she's in the garden," I replied.

"Tell her the taxi's here," The girl said before leaving the room.

I cautiously stepped back outside. The porch light switched on. Sheepskin-Girl was unconscious on the flowerbed. The statues were towering over her, but they stared ahead at me.

Statues should never be sculpted to smile.

Pride And Prophecy,
Andrew Constantinou

"No apologies required; all is well." Mrs. Coleman delivered her line in a high-pitched, throaty and unconvincing tone, accompanied by an icy smile flashed at the man who had nearly spilt the tea he had offered her. As she scuttled away with her husband, her arm locked in his, she yanked him and hissed in his ear: "He is such a fool! If I wanted tea, I would have taken it through my mouth, not my eschelle stomacher!"

Georgiana Coleman was furious, and rightfully so; or at least she thought. Hundreds of pounds were spent on her Parisian gown. To add insult to injury, it had just arrived from Paris that very morning and had nearly been destroyed in a matter of hours! Thankfully, she had the good sense to drag her husband to a photography booth before entering their environmentally friendly automobile. By now, everyone would have glimpsed her new gown on their Instant-Photograph feed. She only regretted being unable to photograph the automobile. Her mouth watered at all the likes she would have accumulated on Instant-Photograph and the wonders an eco-mobile would do for her public image. She herself hated the damned thing of course and would much rather ride in her own fuel powered one. But her husband always rode in the eco-mobile, a symbol of his prestige, as only the wealthiest could afford to do so. Her thoughts turned to the waiter.

"Do you suppose he thought my smile unconvincing?" Horrified at the prospect of being labelled impolite, whilst still hurrying down the hallway, she turned back and flashed a wider smile than before whilst frantically waving goodbye, hoping it would atone for her prior insincerity. It did not, yet her mind was calmed, as her status of the graceful, well-mannered wife of the Prime Minister of Great Caledonia was restored, at least in her head. "Do not concern yourself with such trivial affairs. Ignore him, dear".

Two gloved hands grabbed one handle each and swung the double doors open for the Prime Ministerial couple. As they exited the hall, the Colemans found themselves in the Caledonian Museum's Great Court. Unlike their last visit, sunlight did not seep in through the tessellated glass roof. Innumerable wires prevented natural light from entering the room. The Court would have drowned in darkness if not for the plentiful spotlights at the room's centre, showcasing the object before the circular Reading Room. The couple's echoing footsteps came to a halt, as Aiden Coleman stretched his right arm out, with his palm facing the reason for their visit. "Mrs. Coleman, this is Sophia."

There she was, looming over the Prime Ministerial couple: the titanic head of a Grecian sculpture chained to the ceiling through dozens of wire-shackles. Her once vibrant colours had faded long ago into nothingness, and her countenance had aged into plain, marble white. Upon first glance, Mr. Coleman saw an opportunity: her discoloured complexion was a blank canvas!

Upon his instructions, the Museum's crew painted the sculpture's hair dark red, and what little of her right eye could be seen beneath a gigantic golden cog was navy blue, as was her left. Although her porcelain skin remained untouched, the

Prime Minister felt that cosmetics were required: a dark red St. Patrick's saltire was superimposed above a navy-blue outline of St. Andrew's cross. Both stretched from each corner of her forehead down to each mandible, whilst her nose and the width of her face below her eyes were coated in a dark red St. George cross. Mr. Coleman grinned ear to ear. His personal touch was bound to earn him a roaring reception at the grand unveiling, and the polls.

Sophia had spent the last two millennia atop a gigantic sculpture dedicated to the Greek goddess Athena. The massive sculpture was recovered two-hundred and seven years ago from the former Caledonian colony of Aphrodisia by Lord Moray, its Governor, who had ardently adored it. He admired the sculpture from afar during his frequent visits to an Aphrodisian Acropolis and couldn't fathom parting ways with it upon his governorship's end.

Ergo, as any sensible man would, he took it home with him! The sculpture was eventually sold to the Caledonian Government and ultimately displayed in the Caledonian Museum, where Sophia's former body became a major exhibit known as 'The Moray Sculpture'. Unfortunately, as of recently, The Moray Sculpture resembled more of a massive bust than a sculpture. The reason for this was a mystery. Some accused the Museum of negligence.

Others claimed it a self-destructive act of heartbreak, as the sculpture longed to return under the Aphrodisian sun. Nonetheless, the result was the same: the sculpture crumbled and split in two.

Prime Minister Coleman, whose poll numbers had plummeted to an all-time low, sought to convince the Caledonian public of his government's greatness through the restoration, neigh, the transformation of the Moray Sculpture. Touted as the Caledonian achievement of the Hellenes' ambition, Coleman had transformed a Grecian sculpture's head into an omniscient, encyclopedic robot he baptised Sophia.

"Greetings. My name is Sophia, the Greek word for wisdom. I am named so for I possess all knowledge. I know everything about everything that has ever been, everything that is and everything that will ever be. Possessing all knowledge and sharing it with humanity is my purpose. Pleased to make your acquaintance." Mrs. Coleman's mind clung to Sophia's first two sentences, immediately disregarding the rest as background noise.

"Greek, you say? Oh, the Greeks! What a great civilisation they were!" Her face lit up as she was overcome with pride at what she perceived was a valuable contribution to the conversation. " 'Were' is an incorrect term. The Greeks are an extant community." Georgiana unleashed a glare as cold as the robot's soulless eyes. How dare she correct her? "Yes!" exclaimed Mr. Coleman, unleashing his world-renowned diplomacy. "But they are not so great anymore, are they? Especially when compared to Great Caledonia! Greatness is literally our namesake!" The couple's ensuing irritating laughter was met with a cold blink by Sophia. "Caledonia. A Latin name appropriated from a neighbouring Celtic kingdom you forcibly incorporated into your own." All laughter immediately ceased. "My name," continued Georgiana, "is Greek as well. It means 'Lady of the People', which I suppose given my husband's occupation, is quite fitting." More laughter followed. "Incorrect. Georgiana stems from 'γεωργός', meaning 'peasant'. Whether you consider such a name fitting is entirely up to you." Georgiana's eyes widened. Momentarily, she snatched her husband's arm and spewed her poisonous venom into his ear: "I will not be humiliated by a giant mechanised head!" Following some quiet contemplation, Mr. Coleman responded: "Do you suppose some tea would calm her nerves?" "Chai," chipped in Sophia in her matter-of-fact monotone, "a quintessentially Caledonian custom, imported from Bharat, a former Caledonian colony. Chai is as Caledonian as this room's stone floor, most of which is Gallic." A visible irritation gripped Mr. Coleman, unlike his wife who, relieved at no longer being the subject of scrutiny and having the conversation shift to (what she perceived were) less crucial matters, unleashed a wide, beaming smile.

"Yes, Caledonia has acquired much through her colonies. Yet, her contributions to the world are still great."

"Divisive leadership leading Bharat, Hibernia and Aphrodisia into partition can most certainly not be considered great. Presently, the Anatolian Sultanate strokes the flames of war. Caledonia and her allies have systemically turned a blind eye. You did so as they scorched Smyrna, as the Hayestanis, Hellenes and Assyrians were ethnically cleansed from their Anatolian homes. Now, Syria is the Sultanate's as is half of Aphrodisia. Innumerable lives are constantly lost, human rights constantly violated, yet you turn a blind eye as you did to the Alemannic Chancellor eighty-two years ago."

"Anatolia is a highly valued ally—"

"Precisely. For your Gallic dresses are still delivered, ample money is available for the acquisition of paltry possessions and your nation retains her power and influence, you are perfectly happy with multitudes suffering due to your actions and alliances. Your every choice corrupts everything pure, whether a Grecian sculpture or Mother Gaia. You carve her up, amputate her and watch her bleed. By no means is this a uniquely Caledonian behaviour, rather a common human one reflective of our time. We are now within the Iron Age. Might makes right, bad men use lies to be considered good. Humans no longer feel shame or indignation at wrongdoing. War is your purpose, as always. Man's wickedness is great upon the earth, and his every inclination is evil all the time. And he is aware of this. Humanity has continuously predicted its innate wickedness will lead to its undoing through countlesstales." Refusing to permit a robot best a great man such as himself, Mr. Coleman retorted in a slight vocal tremor:

"If you truly know everything, how does it all end?" The ground spotlights switched off, plunging the room in darkness. Sophia's left marble eyelid sealed itself shut, as blue light beams were emitted through the cog on her right eye.

"Gaia will dance five billion times around Helios before he swallows her whole. Just as he will expand into a colossus and consume her, so will Anatolia devour her neighbours. She will sink her right claw as low as the foothills of Nafusa and as high as the Ruthenian frontier, whilst her left claw will lunge west towards the Vedunian portcullis. The self-proclaimed Five Peace Guardians will instruct their angels, each with multiple incendiary vials, to fly over Anatolia and unleash them upon her.

"Ruthenia will unload hers into Gaia's wound near Kostantiniyye. Her tears will flood the Anatolian peninsula. Columbia will unleash hers upon the Sultan's Seat, resulting in noisome and grievous sores sprouting on the Anatolians, who will gnaw at their own tongues for they have nothing else to gnaw on. Far too preoccupied with Anatolia, Columbia will not notice the Northern Joseonite unleashing his vial upon her, whilst the Indoscythian will similarly attack Bharat. The Caledonian and Gallican vials will make Gaia bleed, and through her rivers shall flow her blood. Her rage for humanity will overcome her. Gaia's head will rumble with anger, as she unleashes her faithful pet serpent to rise and spew poison onto the Aether, further asphyxiating the Anemoi who will already be suffocated by the ash, soot and aerosols birthed by the Guardians' vials.

"A dust blanket will envelop Gaia, hindering the entry of Helios and Selene's light, as Skoll and Hati finally catch their prey. Temperatures will plummet to the depths of Hades, condemning humanity to a never-ending Fimbelwinter and eternal darkness. Helios will grasp for Gaia occasionally, and anyone clutched by him will be scorched. Flora will faun for Helios' touch, yet only a fortunate few will be graced by it, whilst most wither away and along with them, humanity. Merely a third will survive, however, ailed by Helios' absence, they will be plagued by illness. Only a third will survive, with those who do barely resembling humans both in their countenance and manner. Brother will turn against brother, cities and civilisations will be wiped off Gaia's face and Ares will reign supreme.

"Seventy-five millennia ago, Toba gifted Prometheus with the fire to survive the fiercest winter. Yet, man's nature is destructive, and any of his remnants will be destroyed by him."

"Thank you, Sophia. Your words are most invaluable." With a nod of Mr. Coleman's head, a hand in a neighbouring room pulled a switch, and his words were the last she heard. Turning to the registrar, Mr. Coleman barked his orders:

"Limit her knowledge to Grecian myths and delay her unveiling!"

The Colemans exited the Great Court arm in arm. Georgiana's grip however was weaker than before. For the first time, a concerned expression replaced the snobby superiority typically imprinted upon her face. "Do you think any of this shall come to pass?" "Most certainly not! Do not concern yourself with the ramblings of a rogue robot. Ignore her, dear".

ON FALLING IN LOVE WITH YOUR CHILDHOOD BEST FRIEND.
Dylan Davies

"I want to say, 'Mother,
please sit with me in the orange kitchen,
I have something to tell you.'"
—*fragment from "Robert" by Joan Larkin.*

like a magnet dragging a paperclip you and i
moved as one, in synchrony, want-
-ed nothing more than to move to
our perfect rhythm—my mother would say
we were best friends for life—your mother

would say we were soulmates. my mother was please-
-d before she learnt to be scared of the concept. we'd sit
opposite each other in the downstairs hallway with
brooms for oars, practicing our rowing, me
forward you backwards and reversed, in
perfect time, across the wooden river. the

taste of your mouth when we kissed as kids, orange
squash and the good cookies hidden in the kitchen,
running to your garden frog pond to play pretend—i
lag behind to let you win, to have
one guilty look at your long hair. there was something
in the way we tried to meld ourselves together, somehow—to
become the water. i wish i could tell
you this: i could have fucked up with anyone—why you?

ON BEING THE FIRST TO MOVE ON.
Dylan Davies

there's someone else—
we are waiting for my words to reach you—
like your car, your second-hand junk trap slices
out of signal, the radio noise seems to
cut, sputter into quiet,
pass over us completely,
and we remain silent,

waiting. my words are like a wave
that sucks itself back before it floods,
clamps itself on the sandy bank
like a bitten lip, stay seized, and doesn't
come. we are waiting for that
wave, that deluge of white noise,
waterlogged voices muffled by sea;
saltwater gags the talk show—

traffic on the—eastbound going—
now i just don't believe—your own girlfriend—
there's—someone else—

yes   —   here is the radio, choking on
through the salt, voice gurgling outwards,
soaked—your junk trap hurtles into sound,
keeps going, louder—the radio
repeats and repeats, confused by water.
the sea is not enough, the radio cries

there's someone else there's someone else there's—

and my words surge inwards carrying
the same disappointment as rainfall
seeping through half-worn boots,
sodden socks—no tsunami
but puddles, stagnant water.
through the talk show my words foam outwards
bland as traffic—

there's someone—
your mouth opens up and
air bubbles out. the radio falters
in its crying, as if seeking noise,
some reward for not drowning.

the sea, sensing defeat, retracts,
releases your car half-drowned but still
driving. the radio coughs, announces its
news, says that this is a normal day.
the car coughs on, drinking nothing.
neither of us are satisfied.

STAEDTLER® Mars Plastic
Sasha Donovan-Anns

You have made an appointment to degrade a memory. With Helen, you will turn
it into a piece of old film. And then, a piece of old, lost film. She sits opposite in
an armchair that in any other room would be the comfiest chair available. But you get the reclining one, and a blanket (choice of brown or pink) that you usually refuse. Her notes are always taken in pencil, and her swooping words have all the space they need on the unlined sheets of paper. At the start of the session, she takes out your folder, and has a glance at last week's pages. Needing only an overview, you were only asked to tell the story once, and briefly. It took you two years to tell your Mum, and it took two hours with the policeman to pick over every squirming detail of that ten minutes. You are promised that this will be a controlled flashback, and although that's an oxymoron, the scent of lavender brings you a little more forgiveness than usual.

She tells you to pick an image from before and after it had happened.
You don't say anything until you say what you really need to say: that it doesn't feel like it has ever stopped happening. She apologises, because of course that's why you're here, and she rephrases: pick a time afterwards, where the peak of the event had subsided. Then you will have five seconds to get from one to the other. She recommends that you choose some of the key images, images that—

And you're—
      someone walks past wearing his cologne and you feel your throat close, your tongue being dragged back into your stomach
      you are a swallowing fish
      and even in the corridor he forces you down on the sofa again
      cold leather arm on the back of your neck
      running to the bathroom
      inside the cubicle he forces you down on the sofa again
      sticky leather arm on the back of your neck
      and he is above you and he is hard and he knows that you can't breathe, and he smiles
      sticky leather arm on the back of your neck
      and as your body is pushed further off shiny edges
      pushed, pushed, pushed
      the smile above is replaced with the smooth white ceiling
      and you know it's not long now before it finishes,
      before the middle of the ceiling sank as you fainted
      (though your gag reflex will carry on for an hour or so
      after you leave the sofa and the cubicle behind)

yes you know the images. You know them very well. They are the rubble dust that gives lung cancer years after the rescue. Now she seats you in a cinema

chair.
The kind that isn't actually made from velvet, but ensures that you do think of velvet when you sit down. You will watch yourself there, on the stained plush chair, watching the screen. Two steps removed. She counts you down from five and

CARSTANDINGSOFAHANDSNECKSMILEHARDCEILINGHOME

Okay... so it actually was a controlled flashback.
The lavender was right. She counts down again and you

CARSTANDINGSOFAHANDSNECKSMILEHARDCEILINGHOME

You do as she says until she changes what she says.
Next you will imagine it backwards.

HOMECEILLINGHARDSMILENECKHANDSOFASTANDINGCAR

It's strange to see it on a screen bigger than you are. Easier than life size though. Now there's a technical fault, and it's only displaying half the screen. And half again. Until the screen is the size of an apple. You're asked to make it black and white, but that's difficult when you have seen a grand total of one black and white film (six years ago in a substitute teacher dance lesson) which makes her laugh, so she tells you to make it fuzzy instead. You change the lighting so it's green, and it doesn't look so real anymore. You're getting into this, and you can feel the memory curling under your touch. It's more responsive to you, like warmed plasticine. You could roll it out into a cylinder and make a snail. You are making this loop of film into a snail, when she says to take the picture on the screen (you unroll the snail and put it back on the screen) and to drag it onto a piece of paper on a table, so that it looks like a pencil drawing. This is a monochrome image that you can picture more easily. Then you get to rub it out! Rub it all out!

CARSTANDINGSOFAHANDSNECKSMILEHARDCEILINGHOME

CARSTA	INGSOF	ANDSNE	SMI	EHA	DCE	NGHOME
CARST	IN SO	NDSN	SM	EH	CE	NGHOME
CARS	N SO	SN	S	EH	CE	NGHOME
CAR	N	SN	S		E	GHOME
CAR		S			E	HOME
CAR						HOME

The grey littering of the eraser is scattered across the paper and you blow it off. Then you hoover them up, and empty them into a little matchbox. You're allowed to post it anywhere you like. At the end of the session, as you plan your next few weeks, she offers you a tiny cup of apple tea.

You walk your usual route home before tucking yourself into bed. Helen had said that you would process the therapy further when you fall asleep at night, but you're too worn out to wait. Waking up, you try to bring his face into your mind, and you can't. There's a blurry part under his left eye and his nose isn't really there either. It's like he's water damaged, and you think it's about time after all the tears you've cried. But you've felt the need to remember him (avoid him) (fear him) for so long now, that the gaps in his face are more worrying than relieving. You thought you were ready for freedom but instead you search for him on Facebook, and then you're back on the sofa again

> slammed into leather the air is squeezed
> out of your stomach
> and he
> "why are you still trying to get away?"
> elbow at your throat
> the ceiling sinks and you are the drowning one

When you close your eyes the red and yellow patches swarm into the exact angle of his cheekbones. It's like losing your first tooth all over again; who can stop their tongue from probing the gap?

But you go back to Helen to make that gap wider: to rip out all of your teeth and learn how to speak again. You have your images bundled up neatly in dendrites ready for her counting, but this time, in the lavender room, you feel bigger. Almost as if you could be allowed to sit in the comfiest chair in the room, and take a blanket too. The images take you deeper this time, and your right thigh is twitching, your vastus medialis. The memory goes right down into your muscles, into your myofibrils, and your sarcomeres, and their actin and myosin. It's time for him to leave your body now, from the sarcoplasmic reticulum upwards. With every breath out some of the ghostly grease of his fingertips can shed itself from your skin. With every breath in you fill your lungs a little more, and push against the weight of his 6"1 body on top of you. You make him the size of a pea. You make him a helium balloon and you watch it fly through rain clouds. You make him a fly and you swat him. You turn his skin to bubble-wrap and you pop him, bit by bit. She remembers what worked well last time, which is her job, and encourages you to make the images drawn again. You spill tea on the paper. And then you rub it all out again:

CARSTANDINGSOFAHANDSNECKSMILEHARDCEILINGHOME

CARSTA   INGSOF   ANDSNE   SMI   EHA   DCE   NGHOME

CARST   IN SO   NDSN   SM   EH   CE   NGHOME

CARS   N SO   SN   S   EH   CE   NGHOME

CAR   N   SN   S   E   GHOME

CAR   S   E   HOME

CAR   HOME

Now you rip it up, and feed each one to a fire.
Helen's tea is too hot for you to drink. So you pretend to sip it as you come round to the noises outside the room—construction workers, cars, and seagulls. But the warm smell of apple greets your nose and you just breathe it for a while. Breath it so deeply you're tasting it. You're still tasting a little of it on your bottom lip as you say goodbye and leave her house. You'll carry on tasting it when you're home and falling asleep wrapped in your duvet. When you wake up, it will be gone, as will the weight of his torso. Gone. Of course, you will still have the odd fragment, but you don't need to remember it for it to be a part of your story. As a memory, it belongs in the past. It's home now. You belong with apple tea. You belong with the sunrise.

CHOKE
Helen Drumm

Descend from the old brown school bus. Begin walking the long, tree lined road around where you live. Your sister is with you. She has the keys to the house. You lost yours earlier that week. You are prone to losing things. It is nearing winter, and the softly decaying leaves are beginning to freeze into place. You both wear your school uniform. Whatever tights you could find that don't have any holes, whatever white shirt was clean. Your blazer pocket has a hole, which money slips through from time to time. They slide down the lining of the jacket and knock against you. The coins gently ring against you as you make your way along the pavement next to the road.

    You are mostly silent on these walks. This is because when you talk, you fight, and you often lose. You know that mum won't be home for another couple
of hours, and that when you arrive home you will both part and not speak until the morning ride to school. Today, for whatever reason, she will want to have a conversation. You cannot predict the whims of this person, they are as vast and mysterious as the sea. Wonder if she ever really forgets what she has said to you in the past. Wonder if it is perhaps utterly necessary for her to do so. It is lonely and boring, you concede. The silence.

    My sister recounts an anecdote, something about two girls in her year group. Walk on the curb of the pavement. This is ever so slightly closer to the cars moving beside you. This way, you will not brush up against her. Nod and agree and make noises in the right places. Breathe. Later she will make a snack. You will go to your bedroom and wait. When she has closed the door to her bedroom, you will go downstairs. She talks about someone called Beth who is in trouble for piercing her ear with a safety pin in the girl's toilets. She was discovered after having bled all over her English workbook, and playing with the lighter she used to sterilize the needle. Beth has agreed to pierce all the ears of willing participants.
Ask her if she will do the same.
She says maybe.
Ask her whether she is worried mum will see.
She says that she won't.
You feel a twinge in your head. You see the image of the metal gliding through the podgy
flesh of an earlobe.
Tell her it's a bad idea.
She will reply that she does not care.
Say that it will get infected.
She says that this is unlikely if the needle is sterile and she washes her ear every day.
Tell her she's an idiot.
She tells you to shut the fuck up. You are being pathetic.
Bicker with her. She swears at you so sharply that it's like she's poking needles

in you.

Try to keep up, as you are not ready to lose. Her anger comes from a bottomless well. When she was younger she would bite her tongue when she was hitting you or holding you down. One day you pointed it out, and pulled a mocking parody of the tongue. It rolled comically between the bared teeth, brows furrowed and eyes pointed towards each other. Her tongue remained firmly in her mouth from then on.

With one swing, a stick connects with your face. It hits you above your lip and under your nose, where you've begun to be concerned by the light hair growing there. It stings and brings immediate tears to your eyes, and you gasp. Realize she has run off. Touch the tender skin of your lip. Notice that it is split, and that she has the keys to the house.

Now is different. You live alone in a house. The floors are wooden, the wallpaper is a floral pattern. The furniture is not to your taste but is serviceable to your needs. The water, gas, air ventilation and electricity is functional. You suspect that the water is unsafe, but there is not much to be done about that. The windows are boarded.

The air ventilation system ticks like teeth against glass. The upstairs has fallen into itself, and all that is available are the first-floor rooms and the basement.

It is not safe to leave. This is all you can infer from the terrain surrounding the house. The combination of dry forest and relentless heat has created an inferno that has been consuming the area for months. It has turned the sky permanently red.

It is always quiet. You have attempted talking to yourself, singing songs, but your voice can feel strange in the quiet. You have gone through the soundtracks to musicals, summoning characters with clear motives and feelings. You would think that being alone would be liberating, but it's not. You sing with your eyes cast down, and if you cannot reach a note you wince, and the song trails off into nothing. You spend some of your time stretching. You try to keep your body moving. Survival used to be about movement. Whose eyes could spot food the quickest, who could shift quietly through the woods and cut the throat of the beast. Now your survival depends squarely on your ability to stay put. To stay living within the walls of this house. You spend some of your time meditating. This involves breathing and trying not to think about anything. You count your breaths and bring yourself to a state of calm. Sometimes you do this in the 'outside' area. Someone decided to paint the basement an airy blue colour and fill it with fake plastic plants, and when the extra-bright lightbulb is on, it's almost like a summer's day. It is here you have spent many hours, breathing the clean air.

You are so profoundly lucky to have clean air. Boil water on the makeshift stove. You have a small yellow lighter that you use sparingly to perform such tasks. The lighter fluid may run out at some point, and you will have to figure something else out. Wait for the water to boil. Observe the ring of bubbles that collect at the bottom of the pan. Observe the surface as it flickers and erupts. Add coffee granules. Take the mixture off the stove to cool.

Stretch your arms. In the air first, then down to the ground with your feet hip-width apart. Try to touch your toes. You are no athlete, but these are the rituals you remember from your time at school. Your coffee has cooled. Carry it down to the basement room, and switch on the light. Sit down with your back against the wall and sip your drink. There is a meagre bookshelf towards you with a few volumes. There is a particularly dog eared edition of the King James Bible that you have been afraid to open. Pull Alan Moore's Watchmen towards you. Recently, the murky colour scheme and troubling themes have been resonating with you. You have reached the moment where the demented master plan of the mad genious is revealed. In an effort to halt humanity's race towards nuclear war, he convinces everyone that aliens have attacked earth. How? He creates a giant alien octopus with a psychic human brain that transmits nightmares, and then teleports it to New York City, killing half the population. He believes that this is the lesser evil, and indeed the warring global superpowers agree on unity and peace in the face of a larger enemy.

You struggle to imagine anything more horrifying. You wonder what may have happened if someone had intervened in your own planet's race towards destruction. Rorscach walks out into the snow. He will tell the world of the alien plot. He says he will not compromise, even in the face of Armageddon, and you think, what a dickhead. Close the book.

You have begun to feel an acute feeling of despair. You have been alone here for a long time now and are beginning to realize that feeling safe isn't enough anymore. Look up at the bright sky, the clearest, most perfect blue. Look into the sun- a rectangle frame with a long bright lightbulb. Stare into it until you see black spots shimmer before your eyes. You begin to think that you might not move. You might just sit here now. You could just find a way to break the air filter. Eliminate this little pocket from the sea of fire. This way you would be able to sleep with voiceless dreams. The spots dance away as your eyes flutter closed.

Your head rests gently against the wall for a moment.

You hear a noise.

Come forward, as you are not quite sure you heard anything. Again, the bang at the door. Move quickly, lift yourself up, ascend the stairs and run to the entrance of the house.

The banging has stopped.

Wait!

Scream at the door. Slam it with your hand once. Then twice. Then ten in a row. Deep thumps that shake right through your arm to your spine.

Did you imagine it? You cannot tell, but perhaps they're out there on the move. Probably trying another one of the buildings.

Pull your leather jacket and gloves from the cupboard under the stairs, as well as your gas mask. You do not know if it is effective. Attach a pull string, which clips to your belt, connecting you and the house like an umbilical cord. Attach the mask to your face, so much that it should leave red welts later. Your hands are shaking as you pull on your gloves, and it takes you too long to get each finger in the right hole. You do not know that they are enough to protect your skin. Pull the door open and allow the black smoke to enter the house.

The world is chaos, and you are at the centre. Subsumed by a vast cloud of smoke. Everything before your eyes is black. Think of the tiny black particles

passing through your gas mask, into your mouth and down your throat, clinging to the nodes in your lungs. Those same nodes become choked, growing and bulging in strange ways. The air is so hot and thick,
you are hardly getting any oxygen. There is no chance of you calling out or spotting the figure through the haze. Fumble around with your arms, reaching out like a dumbly animated corpse. Under your feet you feel the hard press of concrete. Remind yourself not to slip.
The sun is baking it to a hard crisp. You feel the sweat between your skin and clothes, making the hot material rub and cling. Your eyes feel raw and red, you can barely blink. You ache to take off your mask and give them a hard rub.

 A tug. The chord you have around you has reached all it can. The ring of cord around your waist squeezes, expelling the air in your lungs. There is not enough air around you to sustain the journey back. The ground connects with your shoulder before you can process you are falling. Bones clink together like wind chimes.

 The air is so thick. You feel the concrete move against you like sandpaper, and you realise you are being dragged along the ground. Curl up a little, on your back like an insect, so the hot ground isn't touching any part of you. Wait to be pulled to wherever you are going.

It was after my first death
Isabel Edain

It was after my first death—
It was into the marsh and the silver breath
Of mist that lay over the lake like a corpse—
(Still as a corpse and white as a corpse
Under sky as glass as the eyes of a corpse—)
It was post the peacock-blue sky at the coast
Where small bones of angels and crabs danced like ghosts
And the beach fires sang black as swans' eyes—
It was after the sloughing of miles of self
Of hacking the bindweed that wound to the shelf
Where perched my flowers and darkness—
That I became civilised—I wrote it all down—
And was enveloped by a bright new pelt
(And inside it hid no guts or harebells.)
 My eel-bones retreated—my incisors dropped out—
Human I sat in my quiet pyjamas and wrote scientific accounts.
My sleep was sound; my brain unswelled.
I was perfectly healthy—I perfectly held
My excellent life like a raspberry.
This lasted for months and no-one stopped the clocks —
Time never twisted and halted to watch
A metaphor form like a smoke-ring—
They had filled up my bones with their bright iron nails
They had filled up my boots with their tales of tales
That crawled into girls' brains and sucked them.
So the fey and the ghosts stayed far from my bones
And the tales in the tales were curst from my brain
Spring-cleaned and spring-heeled I ran through the town
Proclaiming my wholeness and absence of pain.

And then—
After the crash-dash—
After ellipses and glittering ash—
That might have been me—that might have been mine—
After the fall—
After the pins crawled out of my bones
And shivered away to the corners of rooms
After the day I took off my boots
And danced violet-toed down into the snow
And the amber witchlight that soaked through the trees
In September—
It was after this, and library books
On raising the dead—on talking with Pucks—

That I slit the throat of that soft summer self
That I burned her hair—I took down from their shelf
The wolves that danced violet-toed in the snow—
That ate glittering ash that once had been mine—
That shivered and quailed because they were mine—

It was then that the leaves came back to their trees
And all the men lay back down in their graves
And tales of tales of tales of tales crawled in through girls' ears
And loved them—
And I am starving—Lady Macbeth—
And calling, darkling, out to my death—
Which waits in the wings of my pet archaeopteryx
Skeletal angel mine—
It is after my first and my third and my fifth—
It is after the fall and after the rift
Through which perhaps we can see (so faintly) the stars—
And time has paused for hours and hours
For I am waiting—with fists full of flowers
That stain my fingers to resemble your eyelids—
Til we sleep the dark sticky sleep of the dead—
Til we sleep with a dark sticky thing like a wasp's nest.

Incarnate
Ally Fowler

This time it is New York City. It has been a week of this new life, and Apollo thinks he is settling in nicely.

It is a city that roils, bacchanalian, where every street intersection offers new exultation—his own brownstone Olympus. After all, he is not one to miss the call of a party when the moon rises and the street-lamps flicker brighter than any constellation he has inhabited. When in Rome, indeed. The Romans never knew such unabashed revelry.

There is a small coffee shop tucked between 23rd and 7th. Apollo stands and waits for his order as the fragments of his life slide into place, tectonic, and the air around his ears is filled with soft chatter. He knows he had complained about wanting things to slow down but in this moment forever seems like too long a wait. The air is thick with steam. Manhattan is sluggish on a damp, grey Tuesday.

"Sir? Your coffee." The barista, a girl no older than eighteen, wide-eyed in consumerist trepidation, interrupts his stupor with quiet caution. She reminds him of the nymphs at Thebes. Apollo takes the take away cup with a nod of thanks and her smile quivers into something a little more-genuine. He sweeps out of the coffee shop and the brass bell jingles lightly in his ears as the door swings behind him. The sound evokes the delicate strings of his lyre, of lazy mornings by the Aegean Sea, lounging on rocks while the rising sun turns his world golden. He pushes down the faint wave of homesickness that makes him shiver.

Apollo has been many things—rotting away in a past life, decadent in an unseen future. He is here and this is now, his same golden curls and olive skin reflected in the passing windows are soothingly familiar. He has been a revolutionary, assembling barricades with bloody hands and bruised feet, taking snarling bullets to the chest because his life was expendable where none others were. He has been a king, with a crown precarious upon his heavy head, callous and harsh when he could have been kind. He has been a carpet maker sweating under a cruel Egyptian sun, spinning golden thread together with neutral tones, marking senseless patterns with sensible wool. He has been young and old. Always a god. Past lives under the same sky; his life a frame narrative, and he will end things as he started them, with the world balanced on the tip of one finger. Power in potentia.

As he turns the corner of the block, he is Apollo and not-Apollo, god and mortal, ichor and blood cells. He is a flicker of static on the television screen, one thing and the other, a quiet distortion. Passers-by spare him no second glances. He will bleed gold and red; that is, if anything could pierce his skin. He is indestructible; a skyscraper in the guise of a man, but it does not bother him too much that he is rendered unrecognisable, stripped of prestige and unceremoniously tossed around, place after place. Apollo has been through this enough times to know that the Fates have their reasons, and he is not the one to know them. Instead he wears time like a cape, flaunting it with jaunty merriment; he is the bearer of second chances and decants nostalgia thick as honey, boyish in his manner but age-old in the lessons learned, forgotten, and learned again.

He is not the only one at the whim of the powers that be. His Olympian family are oftentimes strewn across the world, but it is not rare that some of them end up clumped together. He has seen a few of them over the past few days as he wandered the city, uncommonly idle. New York hides its secrets well, hoarding its gods like precious gold, but Apollo knows enough about treasure to beat it at its game of concealment. Zeus: a harried accounting intern, briefcase in one hand and mobile phone in the other as he hurries to catch the next subway train, eyes stained by shadows like stark bruises, translucent purple on skin. His is a particular fall from grace, and Apollo cannot help the twinge of smugness at the sight of him, their grandiose king stuck at the grinding bottom of life's heap.

Ares: pounding punching bags in a dim underground gym, where the air hums with restless energy and the fluorescent overhead lights flicker with each blow of knuckles to leather. He inhales dust particles and exhales war.

Aphrodite: in a Renaissance painting, tucked in the dusty corner of an art gallery, next to a cracked Grecian urn on a sleek plastic pedestal. Her eyes follow him as he moves to study her, and it is not a trick of the light. Her smile is frozen, seductive and lilting; her hair fans over her breasts, strawberry blonde and curling, but stuck like this, passive, Apollo can recognise none of her.

Oh, well. The thought is bitter. Better luck next time.

Aphrodite blazes through life after life and her husband Hephaestus has a fragile, paper heart, so the Fates carefully catapult them far, far away from each other and pretend that each time it is accidental. Hephaestus is probably on the other side of the world this time, on the shores of South Africa, or Bali, or even Australia, sipping cocktails in the shade of a straw sun hat. Apollo does not mind the distance; he can cross the ocean in a step, and he thinks that the poor guy needs a break every once in a while. He will find him in a near-distant future.

He finds Artemis that same morning, with his coffee in hand and rain on his breath, sitting on a bench in Central Park. It is habit now, forged through eons upon eons (family ringing louder than circumstance, siblings louder than Fate) and they are inevitably drawn to each other like magnets, like the perpetual slide of Archimedes' innovative spheres.

"My favourite sister," he coos, slinging an arm over her narrow shoulders as he slides onto the rickety bench. There is frost on the seat. He knew exactly where to find her.

"Your only sister," she corrects him, frowning as though his sudden appearance is only a mere inconvenience to her. They have played this game enough times to anticipate the conversation, not-hide and no-need-to-seek. He knows she quietly feels the same relief as him, as their two halves slot together again; she is something of an anchor in a sea that does not stay still.

"Careful, now. I could replace you with Athena, or Hestia, if you keep up this cold front." He parodies a shiver and places a long-fingered hand to his aching, restless heart. Quintessential musician's fingers. He did always have a flair for the dramatic.

"You wouldn't dare," she smiles. He returns the gesture, cat-like and languid in the weak January rays of sun.

"How's life treating you?" she asks, fingers tapping idle patterns on the slats next to her leg. He looks her over once, at her hair, dark where his is light, and her eyes, cool where his blaze hot (a perfect familial dichotomy). She wears a jean jacket with faded patches on it, but she exudes the same steely power as when she is swathed in white cotton and golden laurel, hunter's bow strung across her back. Her question is vague but he gets it, he always does.

Apollo shrugs, raises the take-away cup to his lips. "It could be worse." He takes a sip of long-cold liquid and his gaze flickers to the passing taxicabs, yellow and steel, jarring streaks of colour against a grey, grey city. There are stagnant puddles in the road. A beggar on the opposite street corner has his head bowed like a man caught in reverent prayer. "It's a change of pace, at least."

They sit for some while and fill the space with frivolous chatter, with casual observations on who is here and who is not. Artemis swears she saw Hermes modelling Calvin Klein underwear on a billboard in Times Square and Apollo barks a laugh with such force that an earthquake rumbles into life in Northern Japan.

A half-hour eternity later, Artemis is called away and she is whisked into the heart of the industrial beast with only a lingering touch on his shoulder to tide them both over. Apollo sits, contemplates, peels himself from the bench, tosses the paper cup in a recycling bin and hails a cab. He has limited time; he has infinite time. Even he cannot predict his own fate and the city waits for no god. He tells the driver to take him home.

Home is not the address he gives the driver, the address for his apartment quietly collecting dust. Home is where he abandoned his heart last. It has been a few lives since he remembered the location.

GRATER
Chloe Gainford

I

Oh, happiness! What a helium balloon you are. Legs 11; he trots across the dance floor. Abba trickles out the speaker; dancing queen, you're a bit past seventeen. The clean-cut kids are racking lines in the loo when he asks to stay the night. Something bout his momma standing for no more, no more. I wanna say no but tell him I don't want to go home yet. Make some comment about dirty dishes and toenails in the kitchen. He clicks at the barmaid. I sigh. I just don't want him in my bed.

He asks for the jager. Dark and viscous.

He snores in my room. He builds camp in my kitchen, between the mould and mismatched cutlery. He asks why I ignore him sometimes. Then the toast pops up and I shrug and he growls. I look away. He doesn't know where the marmite is kept. I get it myself. I sigh. He, despite the sex - raw and frequent, I barely know. Dark eyes and a smile, he. Shows me a video of some girl I know, vaguely but better than him, having sex at a party. Watch a replay in his eyes; our own private show. Sex tape made? Baby, maybe. I ask about his momma. He shrugs and sparks a fag. Are you lonely? He asks. I tell him frogs can jump 20 times their own height. I tell him the moon landing was fake and stick a cig between my lips. I blow his question into the finite space.

I go back to bed. He heads out the door, leaves the latch on the catch. No pleasantries exchanged. We like it better that way.

II

Some days he comes home, no longer a nameless stranger fluent in the curvature of my spine, and I say nothing because I cannot find the words. He touches me and I flinch. He sighs and I know he wants to snap but doesn't. Just lights a fag and makes some comment about kids these days. He is the calm in the storm of what, upon reflection, is not that stormy of a life. He undresses me with his eyes. I make some excuse and go grab a jumper. The tension deflates like a limp and lifeless balloon. How can something be there and then just not be there?

Tell him about when I buried and lost a locket out in the yard. The thorns grew so sharp and fast. I could never find that bundle again. For years, I looked in every spot imaginable, I'd lay awake at night wondering how I could've missed one. How could something be there and then just not be there?

He says he doesn't know and turns on the television. The static hums and he kisses my neck. I let him and then, between the unwashed, unmade sheets, we have unfulfilling sex. I think it satisfies him but never ask. Communication is key but silence is palatable.

We like it better that way.

III

Nothingness hangs in the air in our apartment, I string it up like colourful balloons above my head. Ask if he bought the wine to take to the party. He doesn't answer, instead making a comment about how I never want to go to parties anymore. Fuck off, I want to say but don't. Instead just say I'm going to fix my make up.

The wine is good and the company is fine but it is hard to enjoy the party through the suffocating depression. That, itself is not the issue, but no one told me depression would bring anxiety. 'Anxiety' being the unwanted cousin from out of town 'depression' was forced to bring to the party.

I am hazy and blurry and he is trying to introduce me to some girl who's name I don't care to know. I smile. I am drunk and sad. I am sighing and crumpling. He wouldn't understand so I just don't tell him. He hands me the jager, dark and viscous. He tells me things are gonna be alright babe and I almost believe him.

Whiskey takes a lot of things out of context so I drink a bottle and then chase it. We stagger home and I tell him that 9/11 might've been a hoax but that I don't really know anymore. He asks me how that could be possible when we saw the planes crash and I sigh because I know that he doesn't know that I know that it is completely possible and plausible for things to be very different to how they appear. Hint about love. I asked him if he could feel it and he couldn't. He just said I was mumbling, drunk silly, and I agreed and kissed his neck because my god was it easier sometimes. He sleeps through the muffled sobs into the pillow that night and though my eyes were red raw in the morning he just doesn't t say anything. I guess we like it better that way.

Iv

Ring, ring, shit! No one ever calls with good news. It's six am and the phone is in the living room. I, though it is in fact a Saturday, am already there. He snores and denies all knowledge. He goes as far as saying i'm dreaming it. He is ridiculous, sometimes. I pick up the phone and I ask who is calling. It's the hospital and they ask for him. He murmurs and he mumbles. His face contorts into the shapes of places I have not been. He ends the call. He is silent. Spark a fag. I pass him the ash tray and ask him what the fuck happened. He says it's something about his momma. How she could take no more, no more. Something about the melodic rise and fall of her chest. Something about how that has faded into the static and her lips must be so blue because isn't that what happens when you die, yeah hun? So sorry, I want to say but don't. I say nothing on the matter in fear of sounding insincere.

V

Oh, happiness! What a helium balloon you are. Legs 11; he shuffles through the busy pub. Wakes are fucking awful he says and I sigh. I straighten his tie. Joni Mitchell on the vinyl, he doesn't know if she would've liked this but fuck it she's dead. Hahaha yeah, that's funny babe. Fucking dark and twisty, eh? The cousins and second cousins and ones who his mum just called cousins are decked in black, getting the next round in when he asks if we can leave. Something bout how his momma, seeing everyone talk about her like this, is too much, too much. I wanna say no but tell him I don't want to go home yet. Make some comment about obligation and needing to take down the table decorations. He clicks at the barmaid. I sigh. I just don't want him behind closed doors.

He asks for the jager. Dark and viscous.

I get a black eye here, a broken rib there. His eyes snarl as he looks for a book, left somewhere between the mould and mismatched cutlery. He asks why I look at him like that now. Why I let him look like he is dying. Then the toast pops up and I shrug and he growls. I look away. He still doesn't know where the kitchen knives are kept, but can always find the liquor. He, despite the sex—drunken and careless, is increasingly violent. Dark eyes and a smile, he. Shows me a video of some girl I don't know, never seen before, his hand on her neck. Watch a replay in his eyes; their own private show. Sex tape made? Baby, maybe. I say nothing. I sigh. He knocks me a punch. Reaches for the frozen peas. I ask how it feels now; without his momma. He shrugs and sparks a fag. Are you lonely? I ask. He tells me it's all just hormones. He asks if I understand. Do you think I'm lonely? I shrug and stick a cig between my lips. I blow his question into the finite space.

I put the peas in the freezer and head back to bed. He heads out to the bar, leaves the latch on the catch. No pleasantries exchanged.

No longer like it better that way.

VI

Emptiness hangs in the air of our apartment, I tug it down and sweep it up with the broken beer bottles. I think about all the lives I am not living too hard for too long and I take a paracetamol. Sigh. He staggers in. Tall and clumsy, he. Shouts some kind of slur at me. Barks something left, something right. Hazy rage. His hands on my neck. His skin, under my fingernails. Bangs me up against the wall. Concussion? Baby, maybe. Undresses me with more than just the eyes. Fragile, I. Think about how he said nothing when my skin started changing colour. Think about how I saw it just like the pageant of the seasons, ever evolving.

Blink. Don't scream you'll scare the neighbours. Blink. Are you sure you want to have all that skin on show? Blink. Bottle by the bed. Night cap, he says. He rises like the sun, eyes bleary. Appears slightly smudged, he. Grabs a bagel from the fridge. Complains about the lack of cream cheese and my latest promotion. Leaves work at lunch time, heads to the bar. Rinse. Repeat. Drunk again, he swings through the door. I sigh and I cry. His hand. My face. Contact made. Collateral damage, I. Look through photos in the attic, find ones of his momma. Sigh because I too can take no more, no more. Catch myself in the mirror.

Prop my feet up on the bath. Pray he doesn't catch me. Set the timer. Lean against the wall. Tick. Two minutes. Tock.

Pick up the stick, pink lines on the tip. Shit.

He, despite the sex—aggressive and unwilling—I barely know anymore. He, a father? No, I'm not ready for. Him in those baby photos, bright blue eyes and a smile. Him, stumbling through the door, red cheeks and furrowed brows. Him. His hand is bleeding. Crimson red and stinging. I see our baby's fingers curling around those knuckles. I see our toddler confusing beer bottles for breast milk. I think about those pink marks on the stick and how they almost mirror ones he has left on my skin. Early, that night he goes to bed. Shuts the door. Turns all the lights off. This is the last time he ever sees me.

Somehow it's just better this way.

VII

When my daughter asks about her father, I'll keep the details hazy, like all those red hot nights. I will tell her about those duck egg curtains and the hairpin curve of his lips. I'll talk about all the running away times, those when we actually happy as apposed to just saying we were. Sigh.

I get up for night feeds. I think about how he will never hold a piece of himself between his arms and gently rock it to sleep, how he will never get to teach her to ride a bike or go kart or kayak. I think about how I thought he'd be the only person i'd ever love, like actually love, not like the way you love your Aunt Lou because your weird mother says you have to. I think about how I was wrong. How, as our daughter takes her first steps, I watch a phoenix rise from the ashes. I think about him, about how I only ever miss him sometimes.

He; a distant memory of what only ever sort of was. I don't write, he doesn't call. Too busy chasing the (actually corporate) corporate job. Too busy kissing midnights and looking down the bottle.

I know it's just better that way.

Seventy Million Tills
Sebastian Gale

Winter
boots,
Dawn.
The lonely doorway of a café.
Lips are purses, tight-grip and hard-bit on coppers not seen,
seldom smiling, spitting contributions
at the homeless, and at their dogs.
Night-time
tickets,
Waiting.
Silence between strangers and stops.
Portraits from the darkness where buses pass by,
window-to-window, scenes of life lit up with filaments;
love, money, reality TV,
all sorts of small hopes and tragedies.
Hot
sound,
Spare cash.
Five pence for plastic bags.
These myths and legends have no taste,
like cocaine on a fiver, in and out of
tills in seventy million lives,
all spread thin between Waitrose and Costco.
It's the only myth to outlast
its maker.

NOTES TO A YOUNGER SELF...
Emma Goodyear

they say you do you
but if they knew they'd see
not me
but it
with all the connotations and misconceptions
that taint all those who
stand out
whatever reason that may be
eyes always upon me
even if no-one is there to see
paranoid delusions breed obsessive illusions
senses never stop tingling
them and I
immiscible intermingling
never singling out
any thought that would cast doubt
on the fanciful façade that is me

I wish I'd heard somebody say
someday being you will be somewhat okay
I'm down but not out
clipped wings warning markers
have damaged my span
but I'll beat back again
shit hits the fan but I rise like a phoenix
shout fire in my cries
I am not a moth but a butterfly
watch me fly high
wear my colours with pride.

Longing
Emma Goodyear

ethereal goddess
with her wisps and her crisp
morning spring in her step
her air iconised in her ocean deep eyes
heavenly halo strands fall grandly cascading
beauty pervading with delphic reserve
catch every curve as she moves
a celestial turmoil
an unhealthy addiction

throw caution to the wind
spread your wings for your thunderbird moment
brief sense of atonement
glide towards salvation
make your heartfelt confession
in the hope that behind those cerulean eyes
is a glimmer of familiar tiptoeing motions
and misplaced assertions
but end up collaging those
sharp pink shards
somehow survive each incessant mirage
and again you know
it is not to be

My Illness Has Teeth
Samuel Gordon Webb

Espresso. Single. Yep. Thanks.
11:32. Busy. Ish. Quiet. Ish. Coffee grinds, occasionally. There's a dilemma fidgeting with my soul. It's killing me. A little. Slowly. Not much. Slowly. It's like a pulse, beating,
more, and more, and more. I cough twice, but I am fine.
Trust me.
All good.
Trust me.
Nothing bad.
Trust me.
My dentist would kill me if she saw me here, destroying my teeth, but she's not, so she can't, so I am safe, for now. I think. But yeah, fine, fine fine.
Debby Kanter. PhD in dentistry. Green eyes. Flat nose. White teeth. Obviously. Her breath stinks of wild berry freshener. Her veins look like vermicelli noodles. She drinks hot water. No Coke. Never. No sweeteners. Never. No sugar. Never. No complex carbohydrates after 8pm. Never.
Her hair is a stiff depression. Subdued. Horribly subdued. And washed. Ferociously. Like a mannequin. She wears orange socks. Not sure why. But she does. And she smiles, because I don't. She smiles a lot, not happily, but knowingly. Like a witch. Uhh.
She asked me to keep a tally of the number of cups of coffee I drink per day. I keep the tally in my mind. 3 so far today, I think. If decaf counts, then maybe 4 or 5. If the green tea counts, then 5 or 6. Pushing 7. Maybe. I'm predicting 3 or 4 more. I sense a coffee splurge. Somehow. In the air.
Today the coffee is Columbian. Yesterday it was Kenyan. The day before that it was Turkish, or Pervuian, or Ethiopian, although it tasted Guatemalan. I wonder if they grind the beans on site. I wonder who grinds them? I wonder if it's worth looking into. I wonder.
Debbie hates my teeth. My teeth hate Debby. Coffee hates my teeth. I can feel yellow rust on my teeth. Coffee must blister your heart, declare war on your soul before leaving a rigorous legacy in your mind.
Debby always asks me if I brush my teeth. Yes, I do, twice, daily. Obviously. Duh. Electric toothbrush? Yep. Obviously. Duh. Floss? Yep. Obviously. Duh. How exactly do you brush? Sideways? Up and down? Neither? Both? I don't know. I don't care. Sideways. Sideways. Sideways. I say. Always. She says "I hope.. I really do hope things pick up".
Pick up is her favourite phrase. Things always need picking up. Somehow. Dirty teeth gives her something to do. Surely? Cleaning up the dirt? Surely? Like a police officer. Like a domestic cleaner. Like an embalmer. She cleans the mess up. Surely?
Recovery is worth it.

I am going to construct a story from the medium sized kid in blue track pants, waiting at the walk signal. He will fast until 10pm, eat ice cream for 3 hours, go to bed feeling sad, wake up and drink coffee until 10 pm, then his breath will

stink of copper. His heart will sleep on coffee. His brain will swim in coffee. He will survive the night. He will buy more coffee in the morning.
Is he ok?
Dad always says nobody is ok. Dad hates the word normal. He calls me eccentric instead. I disagree with my dad. I am normal. I dress normally and I do normal things. I have normal attributes and I have normal thoughts.
I wrote 4125 words in 21 minutes on Russian intervention in Syria on Christmas Eve. I need to know about the world. I need work to feel good. Like normal people. People work. People get money. People feel happy. Most people. Yeah? Normally. I like normality.
The guy near the cash register looks like he's been swimming in the Hudson. He's deciding between coffee or juice. His left eye moves faster than the right, totally weird, strolling the menu. Still deciding. Still deciding. He orders fruit rooibos, oatmeal with fruit compote, no syrups, no nuts, cooked in milk, almond milk, I think.
He pays with his card. It's declined. He tries again. It works. The receipt bleeds out. The oatmeal takes a while to heat so he slowly paces around near the washrooms. I feel bad for the floorboards. Plain oatmeal for Dave? Yep, he grips the cup, thanks very much, and now he runs off like a burglary gone wrong. My bones shudder.
Did I frown?
I think, not sure. The woman next to me is frowning. I am trying to keep myself to myself. I feel her eyes on my neck, like a needle scratching. My collarbones twitch. I avert my gaze to the dust storms happening on the floorboards.
I enjoy watching dust dancing. I step back. A while back. I am riding camels in Saudi Arabia. I ate 15 dates. I didn't count. I probably ate more like 20. I didn't count. Not then. Nothing counted. Nothing mattered. The whole desert fizzed. Really. It did.
I told Debby. She didn't believe me. I showed her my ticket to Riyadh. She still didn't believe me. Debby never believes me. She only believes what she sees. This feels wrong to me. Very wrong. Highly frustrating. Ridiculous. My feet tingle. My arms spasm, my chest pumps liquid to my throat.
The wrong way?
Coffee makes you jumpy. I just ordered a double shot. I do everything to please Debby. Except what she asks of me. It makes me feel powerful, to deny her like this. It's my power to choose. Power makes me happy.
My double shot just arrived. I got a free biscotti on the side, so I created a smile using my knowledge of what smiling looks like. I show my teeth. I hold this expression for 6 seconds.
The coffee roams my body like a pacifist. I am already bored.
I get cramps in my left leg, like frying shallots in butter.
It caramelises in my feet.
I could go home now and eat pasta with my family.
I could, but. Well, coffee keeps me, here, dreaming. Not sure why.
I will open my own wine bar in Brooklyn and it will be called Glass of Words. I will write 12 books and 3 will be shortlisted for the Man Booker Prize.
I will marry the waitress I see at a pizzeria in LA. We will propose underneath the fig tree in my garden. My parents will watch from the window upstairs. Mum

will cry and dad will squeeze her shoulder. They will look proud. So proud. My dog will bark.

We will eat salmon en croute for lunch, then rhubarb crumble with coffee ice cream. I will make a joke about the past. Everyone will laugh. I will. I will. I promise. Give me time. I promise.

My phone is 2 % charged.

I have 14 miscalls and 12 new messages.

Debby rang twice at 11 AM.

I lower the brightness to 25 %, less fierce, more subtle, a little, not much, but enough, enough to see my face on the screen, a tiny thing, rocking, slightly, losing shape, a little,

not much, coming, going, coming, going, like a ghost,

there, not there, there, not there,

there, there, there.

Your Two Minutes Hate
Alex Grenfell

Yellow rags, paper devils,
Fib about invisible rebels
Trampling over freedom's blood
To welcome a foreign flood.

Fabricating flimsy Parliament
Tyrannised by enemies sent
To chain England to Europe
And have Great Britannia stoop

To continental bureaucrats.
See, they call refugees rats
While printing naked pictures
Of half-dressed celebrity strippers,

While conducting ruthless crusades
To embolden their civic charades.
Brainwashing boomers and leavers
Till they become believers

In farces like Muslim no-go zones,
Soya altering men's hormones,
Markle's demonic possession,
The notion that depression—

Like Tommy's guilt—is a falsehood,
That half-brained millennials would
Kill themselves for profiles on phones,
Someday will buy their own homes,

That migrants daily sneak onto our shores,
That these actresses are all whores,
Boris will bring holy Brexit
And is not another hypocrite,

Russia our friend and ally,
That the apocalypse is nigh,
Baptise party leader terrorist,
News as fake, left-wing and errorist.

This toilet paper, these red-tops,
Nazi props littering corner shops,
Owned by Murdoch, greedy master,
Leading England to disaster,

Misinform our populace,
Till we are a global disgrace.
Direct our kings, leaders, laws,
To let our freedoms die with applause.

In your grandparents' living room, aged seven

Oliver Hancock

You, reading fairy tales to endless parrot chatter,
Crooning noises from behind newspapers, begging for lunch.
Your grandfather, smoke ringed sighed reply, your grandmother's
Clock tutting, ticking at the crossword and gnawing pencils.
Bubbling soup and fountain and fish-tank, do not drink
From it you are not a dog, where's the dog? Your fingers
Tracing aboriginal myths in the rug, crocs and macaws
Tickling your toes. Go and wash your hands, Uncle's name,
Dad's name, your name. Your name, tangy, like copper.
Did you wash your hands after pennies? You, slurping,
Do not slurp your name, Dad's name. Say thank you.
Sitting, watching the fountain, feeling fingers in your hair
And listening to trickling 'I love you's. Dust on everything.

Conscience
Oliver Hancock

You should not talk to strangers at 3am
In dark alleyways of cities you have not visited before.
Direct your gaze anywhere but their eyes, and refrain
From a slurred come with anyone tonight?
It is wise to avoid breathing a night of tequila
Into your companion's face, but wiser still
To offer them a cigarette in recompense.
Try, if you can, not to sway along to Believe
Echoing from a door nearby. Try, if you can,
To preserve some decorum, some self-respect.
Eschew desire from watching moustachioed
Lips suck on the slim you've given up, and absolutely
Do not step closer and put your boot by his.

Do not lean in, do not swap breath.
Direct your attention to the skeins of smoke
Flirting with neon above your heads; forgo
The possibility of waking between strange sheets.

An anonymous SpaceTripAdvisor® review of 'Planet Earth'

Ida Hansen

(inspired by Craig Raine's poem A Martian Sends a Postcard Home)

I was clearly not the first visitor
Other species have colonised this blue orb
I think it would be unwise to mingle in their affairs

A strange giant roams these lands
Its growl can be heard from afar
I've seen it swallow twenty earthlings whole
Lined up for execution
One
by
one
Then it fled the crime scene with a roar
Only to be haunted by regret
And spit them out again

A hard-shelled parasite also feeds on the earthlings
Attached to their hands
It mumbles softly in their ears, or shouts and screams
And they answer
Sometimes it goes quiet
And they stroke it intimately with their thumb while it's sleeping

The earthlings wear layers of colourful armour during the day
even though no one fights each other
Yet after nightfall they shed all defences
and have gruesome one-on-one wrestling matches
on padded battle fields
sweating and screaming in pain

It makes my tongue hairs stand on end

I can't wait to get back home
I see no reason to return to this planet
Please spare yourself the trouble
2/10 stars

Keeping Company
Kasper Hassett

'Have you met Upstairs yet?'

Aunt Ruth had got up from the sofa—an ugly, dark floral two-seater with worn away seats. He perched on the stool he had brought from home. He eyed the sofa, unconvinced that it was not already claimed by millions of microscopic bugs. The smell of damp curled through the air occasionally, wrinkling his nose.

'Uh… No, not really.'

'Not really?' she said. 'What do you mean not really?' She had wandered to the kitchen alcove. Her walking was heavy and slow; her weight was shifting from one stiff leg to the other; her arms were poised to start running. His mouth opened, closed, and opened again silently. 'Oh, Tony, I can't find the coffee.'

'I don't have any coffee,' he said. 'And, I've heard Upstairs, but I haven't seen them. Shuffling around, turning the tap on, that kind of thing.'

She grimaced. 'Why don't you have coffee?'

'Don't drink it.' He looked away.

'Stupid boy you are!' She started rummaging through sugar, teabags. 'You need to have coffee for when people come over.'

Tony squinted. Aunt Ruth's voice had been ingrained in his memory from the recent phone calls. It had been a week and five days since he moved, and most days she messaged, half the days she phoned. 'How are you settling in?' she asked at the beginning of each call. Then, another question, more specific: 'what food have you got in?' or 'used to getting around?' or 'are you mopping up the condensation every morning?'. One day it had been 'have you heard from your dad?', but Tony did not think she would try that again. He had said 'no' and the two had been caught in a painful silence for an everlasting minute, broken only by the crackling of the air down the line.

Why did the air find a voice only on the phone? Tony wondered.

Aunt Ruth had come with groceries. Much of it was predictable—bread, milk, apples, spinach, potatoes (what am I supposed to do with a whole sack of the bloody things?), eggs and carrots. Some of it was stranger, and Tony did not know what to do with it—flour, tinned mushrooms, a plastic sack of ice. There was a bottle of slightly-pricier-than-cheap white wine, which she declined when Tony offered a glass of it. She had not brought coffee.

She left when she had run out of things to say. It was almost automated—she had come with a purpose—food to deliver; corners to inspect; nosiness to satisfy. She had kept a bank of questions, similar to those in the phone calls, which fed into the nosiness. She would report back to his father, Tony thought, and his father would consider this report, nodding in his imposing armchair, satisfied that the thing he had created was still breathing.

He saw her out to the car, which waited patiently at the bottom of the narrow front garden. 'Thanks for coming,' Tony said, offering a hug.

Aunt Ruth's hug was tight and drawn out. 'Anytime, darling. Keep yourself well.'

The door next to Tony's swung open. They stopped, went silent, and watched as a slender middle-aged woman emerged, a satchel smartly swung over her shoulders.

Her hallowed cheeks supported watchful brown eyes, lucidly moving around the eyeballs yet unchanging in state. Her satchel and leather jacket were adorned with badges, and her tufty hair was short enough to reveal spiked earrings. She eyed them, and cautiously stepped past, letting the damp gate hang limply behind her.

They stared after her for a minute, as she took off towards the high street. Aunt Ruth, who had been breathing audibly, turned to Tony.

'Did you see? She was another one – you know – like you!'

*

The tenant before had fled, Tony was told. She was deep in debt and left the place in an absolute state, the landlord, a snide little man who lived in one of the picturesque northernmost boroughs, had said. 'It was disgusting, you should have seen it. But it's all been cleaned up and renovated just for you,' he boasted, slipping in a sweeping glance up and down Tony's whole body. The glance said, 'it's cleaner than you deserve', and it imagined him stubbing out cigarettes against the wall.

Tony did not smoke. The little man from Barnet or Camden or Enfield cradled and rubbed his ring finger when he walked, though there was nothing on it but a fresh indentation of red flesh. He had waltzed down the front path after saying this and handing him the key, past the bin he shared with Upstairs, and dropped into his car. Seeing him on the path had irritated Tony, like the magic of his new home was stained with the memory of the landlord's smug, closed-eyed nod.

*

The tube whisked him to Central. He realised he could invite old friends, then realised he did not want them there. The memory of the summer solstice was burning into flesh on every unshaded street, and the sky had started softly turning pink at 8pm. He had eaten dinner, but found himself in a Chinatown bakery: flavoured bread and sweet treats lined the shelves, and before even thinking, he had bought a melon pan and was wandering down the street, clasping it through the crinkling plastic wrapping. It tasted like bread. Tony had never been able to pick up on subtlety.

The sky darkened, and he found himself adjacent to the clubs in Soho as their doors were opening, low glows emanating from their depths. He stepped from the twilight into a dark, musty room. The first club was empty, but he drank, quickly, enough to let him sway to the least popular of the music that would be played that night. The DJ eyed him with suspicion from across the wide space, looking away when their eyes met.

He moved on. He roamed from club to club, eyes hunting for people. As the district became more populous it occurred to him that he had been moving through the club doorways without checking what they were called, and sometimes he did not hear the bouncers, their voices lost in seas of drunken squeals. He entered a dark room filled with smoke and sweaty bodies and intermittent green flashes. It was enough to blind someone, but the intoxicated bodies writhed lapsing from time with the bass shaking the building.

He danced with a man, somewhere around the sides. He could not hear the man's name, but he nodded at it. "I'm Ant," he replied.

Ant did not want the other man to talk. He had an ugly, hoarse voice under the music, and he spat with some words. He was too imposing, too tall, too closely angled towards him. Ant used the rhythm as an excuse to create space between them. The man wanted to go home with him. Alone, Ant slunk into the dark-corners and through the night.

Ant stumbled through the gate. It was 4am. The lights were on above his studio flat, and as he entered he switched on a flimsy lamp and the television, muted. He watched figures mouthing phrases he could not read on the screen, his own music floating around the room instead. He pulled the cork from aunt Ruth's bottle of wine, poured a glass.

The reflection of the television screen chattered against the window. Ant lay back into the ornate sofa, his head nested on the lumpy backing. Through a thin ceiling he heard Upstairs clinking a bottle against a glass. He laughed. 'Cheers' he said, lifting his glass, 'to the lonely bastards like us.'

Outside, the air was silent.

Yours Alone
Maddi Hastings

Your lips must be starved, chapped and aching,
With soft picks they'll sip the blush from her skin.
A little fever keeps your mind in wanting
And trembling. This love's now breaking in.
You shed your skin and leave it at the door,
Caught in thoughts that mark her as yours alone—
To have, to hold, to tear apart and adore
Where her imperfections are said to roam
Within her patterned hide—so bitter it is
In your teeth. The tissue shed from you both
Spread across the carpet as flesh kisses,
Left together to fester as a single growth.
I know she's close to you, lying in bone,
These lingering scraps of you, once mine, she owns.

THE EGG
SIOBHAN HORNER-GALVIN

FADE IN:

IN BLACK AND WHITE
EXT: #1 SUFFOLK SKY - LATE AFTERNOON

We see the sky with a few, low clouds. Total silence. Then the low rustle of a light breeze in the trees.

TITLE IN:

2039

EXT. #1 -MELTON STREET - LATE AFTERNOON

We see the back of a small, dark-haired boy in school uniform running down a residential street. We hear the sound of heavy footsteps in pursuit. We hear the boy panting.

BULLY #1 (O.S.)
Oi! Get 'im.
(shouted loudly with aggression)

We see the boy run cross a road between electric cars. The car honks its horn. The boy disappears into some woods. We see three bullies (one chubby, one tall and one small with a dog) make chase across the road. As the chubby-bully gets to the woods the bully-with-dog pulls him back by his sweatshirt. The chubby-bully stops, panting, red in the face.

CHUBBY BULLY #1
Wha—

BULLY WITH DOG #2
Just leave 'im.
(said in Suffolk accent)

Bully 2 crouches down and fusses over the dog.

CHUBBY BULLY #1
Yer bleedin' soft Billy, yer bastard. You 'n yer bleedin' animals.

The chubby-bully punches the bully-with-the-dog on the arm. They stare into thick woodland, trees and undergrowth.

EXT. #2 - SUFFOLK WOODLAND - LATE AFTERNOON

We look up at the sky through the greening branches of the trees, and then back to earth—a pair of boy's legs in muddy shoes are crashing through the undergrowth. We hear his shallow breathing. We see him look back for the bullies. He trips over a fallen branch and crawls to the tree stump to hide. We hear only the boy's breathing and the shuffle of leaves as he gathers them and wipes the mud from his shoes. We see him suddenly stop. He stares intently at something by the tree. It is an upside-down bird's nest.

RAVI #3
Woah
(whispering)

He turns over the nest to reveal a lone egg. He takes great care, his fingers turning over the egg. He stares at it. It is grey-green with a yellow underside. It is the only colour in the scene.

RAVI #3 (CONT'D)
Woah
(whispering)

The boy puts the egg to his ear and listens. He suddenly recoils from it. He puts it back to his ear.

RAVI #3
Woah

Ravi picks up the nest and places the egg inside. He tugs some grass to nestle the egg and, cradling the bundle under his coat, he hurries off out of the woods.

EXT. #3 - BACK GATE LEADING TO BACK YARD - EARLY EVENING

Ravi pushes open a back gate into a small yard, then a back door into a small kitchen-diner.

INT. #4 - SOCIAL HOUSING HOME, EARLY 2000 STYLE: PATTERNED CURTAINS AND SCUFFED CARPETS. NET CURTAINS. KITCHEN SPARSE - EARLY EVENING

Ravi glances around the kitchen-diner. He looks at the clock. It is four fifty.

O.S
(sound of tv on loud, a game show)

RAVI #3
Gran?

O.S.
In here, nene.

INT. #5 - SITTING ROOM - EARLY EVENING

Ravi peers round the doorway. He looks around as though he's checking for someone. An old Indian lady is sat on a sofa, knitting and watching tv. She looks up, frowns.

GRAN #4
Not again.

Ravi stands by the door and nods.

GRAN #4 (CONT'D)
Those two are badamash.
But...Shane? Tct.I know his nan.
(shaking her head)

Here, have a butterscotch.
Gran holds out a sweet. Ravi takes the nest from
under his jumper and holds it out.
She drops the sweet, gasps, her eyes wide. She holds her hands out.
She looks worried. She darts a look at the windows that face the street.
GRAN #4 (CONT'D)
Go pull those curtains. And lock the back door.
RAVI #3
But
GRAN #4
Go!
(firmly)
The boy draws the curtains and leaves the room.
Gran tilts her head back, holding the nest.

IN BLACK AND WHITE
EXTREME CLOSE UP OF GRAN'S FACE

Gran's eyes close.

CUT TO:

EXT. #5 - SUFFOLK MARSHES WITH BIG, OPEN SKY - DUSK.

There is full colour, a pink dusky sky, streaks of yellow and blue in the sky. Classical music. A murmuration of starlings swirls and swoops in the sky. There is an overwhelming sound of birds chattering.

MUSIC CUE: Vaughan Williams: The Lark Ascending (1914)
O.S. (RAVI'S VOICE)
Gran?
MUSIC END.
CUT TO:

EXTREME CLOSE UP OF GRAN'S FACE

Gran's eyes flick open. The music stops. All is
quiet. A tear rolls down Gran's cheek.

INT. #4 - SITTING ROOM - EARLY EVENING
RAVI #3
Gran?

(sounding worried)
Gran's dabs at her tear. She sniffs. Ravi stands in
front of her. She cradles the nest.
GRAN #4
I haven't seen one of these in...well...too long.

Gran grabs Ravi's sleeve.
GRAN #4 (CONT'D)
Don't tell Daddy. He'll make us turn it in. We've got to hide it and
RAVI #3
Why, what is it?
Ravi sits down on the sofa, up close to Gran, eyes darting to the windows.
GRAN #4
It's an egg.
Pause. Gran and Ravi stare at the egg.
RAVI #3
What's an egg?

TITLE OVER: A WEEK LATER

EXT.#6 - FRONT DOOR OF RAVI'S HOUSE IN MELTON - MORNING

Bully-with-dog is ringing the doorbell and shifting on his feet, looking behind him. The doorbell doesn't sound. He turns to go. The door opens.

GRAN #4
It's you. Shane, isn't it?
BULLY-WITH-DOG #2
Um...is...um...is Ravi there?
Shane looks sheepish, eyes lowered to the ground, hands playing with the dog lead. Gran opens the door and lets him in.

INT. #3 - KITCHEN - MORNING

We hear the local radio on in the background. Dad, Gran and Ravi having puris for breakfast. Gran slops paneer onto a puri and passes it to Ravi. Dad drinks his tea.
RAVI #3
You ever seen a bird, Dad?
DAD #5
Don't be daft. Your gran will have though.
Dad stuffs a puri in his mouth, turns to Gran.
DAD #5 (CONT'D)
Remember birds?
DAD #5 (CONT'D)

Birds? You know...
(he is speaking very loudly)
Dad makes a flapping motion with his arms. He looks over to Gran.

GRAN #4
I'd like to see a bird again...before I—
DAD #5
Worth a fortune now. Remember Geoff from number forty-two? Handed in a starling a few years back. He lives in Spain now
The doorbell rings. Gran looks at Ravi. Ravi looks away. Dad goes to the door.

INT. #7 - INSIDE FRONT DOOR AND HALLWAY - MORNING
We see the hallway from Ravi's point of view, looking towards the front door at Dad's back are two men in uniform. They are mumbling. The men point towards Ravi and Dad turns.
We see Ravi click the kitchen door quietly, grab his coat from the hook by the back door.
RAVI #1
It's them.
(whispering)
Gran passes Ravi the egg from her knitting basket. She places her hand over his and holds it there just a fraction longer. Ravi puts the egg in his coat pocket. Ravi hesitates. Gran passes him a puri.
GRAN #4
Go!
The back door closes. We hear the sound of the latch on the gate. Gran locks the back door and sits down to another puri.

EXT. #1 -MELTON STREET - MORNING

We see Ravi from the back, running down the street.
O.S.
Stop! Just stop. Don't make it worse than it already is.
We see Ravi turn to look back at his pursuers. It is the men in uniform. Ravi turns a corner and runs straight into the bully-with-dog.

EXTREME CLOSE UP
Ravi looks up at the bully-with dog.

EXT: #1- MELTON STREET - MORNING

We see the men in uniform turn the corner onto the street and we hear the sound of their heavy footsteps in pursuit. We see them run up to the bully-with-the-dog.

MAN IN UNIFORM #6
You seen a boy run this way?
The men in uniform indicate Ravi's height. The bully boy points to the wood.
BULLY #2
Yeah, he wen' in there.
MAN IN UNIFORM #6
C'mon. Spread out. He won't get far.
We see a close up of the BULLY 2, cradling something in his sweatshirt.

EXT. #2 - SUFFOLK WOODLAND - MORNING

We see Ravi's shoes pounding through the undergrowth and hear him panting. We see him scramble over fallen logs and run on through undergrowth. We hear the men in pursuit, shouting.
MAN IN UNIFORM #6
Give it up, kid. We've got you surrounded.
Ravi turns to look behind him. He stumbles, trips and falls. (SLOW MOTION) Silence. We see the trees and the sky. We see three men in uniform standing over a body. We see Ravi facedown on the ground, surrounded.
MAN IN UNIFORM #6 (CONT'D)
Turn out your pockets, then.
We see Ravi's pocket. There's a stain growing on it.
MAN IN UNIFORM #6 (CONT'D)
Shit!
MEN IN UNIFORM #7 AND #8
No! No! Fuck.
Ravi opens his pocket. We see inside. It's one of his Gran's puris, the gooey, white filling oozing out of his pocket.
MAN IN UNIFORM #6
What the...?

EXT. #4 - SUFFOLK WOODLAND WITH BIG, OPEN SKY. - DUSK.

We see two boys crouched by the old tree stump, heads leaning in towards each other. A small dog is held close to one boy.
RAVI #1
Look!
Ravi pulls the boy's sleeve and the boy holds his dog back.
The dog whines and tries to press forwards.
BULLY-WITH-DOG #2
Feck! What the-?
The chick pecks at the egg and we see a beak appear, then a head, some wings and a tiny body, sticky with feathers.
RAVI #1
You can't tell anyone. If they find it they'll want to keep it, and Dad'll just want the money. Gran says as soon as it can fly we'll have to let it go, somewhere far out of town,

and then maybe it can find another one, and—
BULLY-WITH-DOG #2
Can I hold it?
The boy picks up the chick and holds it in his
cupped hands, grinning in wonder.
RAVI #1
Gran said the sky used to be filled with them. Birds.
BULLY #2
Birds.
RAVI #1
Thousands of them in great flocks, swirling about
the sky every single night, looking for a place to nest...
BULLY #2
We'll be the ones who brought the birds back.
FADE OUT TO BLACK. SOUND OF BIRDSONG FROM GRAN'S
DREAM.

MUSIC CUE: BIRDSONG RADIO - THE TAKEOVER

TITLE IN:
BRITAIN HAS LOST 40 MILLION BIRDS IN THE LAST 50 YEARS

TITLE IN:
PROTECT THEIR NATURAL HABITAT.

FADE OUT.

THE END

Rollicking Randy Dandy Oh.
Charlie Humphreys

Father had always wanted to be a sailor. At the dinner table, his conversation was of the sea, and of his dismay when, during the war, he'd been drafted into the Army rather than the Navy. He made up for it post 1945; after settling into the family business he bought himself a cruising yacht. He christened it *Marilyn*. In later years, I broached the question as to why, and he told me it was because of his fondness for the films of Ms. Monroe. Mother had nothing to say on the matter. During the summer holidays when I was back from school Father would make a habit of taking Sissy and myself out on the water in *vt*. Those were fine days; my older sister and I sitting on the side, orange life jackets over our summer clothes and our legs dangling in the North Sea. There's one picture I have of Father; shirt sleeves rolled up, a pipe sticking out of his mouth, and a captain's hat perched on his head at a jaunty angle. Behind him you can see the sun settling behind the horizon. It's a rather majestic shot, like what one might find on the side of a tin of pilchards.

Father was usually so busy in the office we never got to see him. I treasured these expeditions with a man who, day to day, I saw as a stuffy old businessman. When the sea was on his mind, he transformed into a jolly sailor. We'd look forward to the knock on our bedroom door in the early morning when he'd rush in with calls of "Ahoy shipmates!" We'd don our raincoats and scurry out to the car. In open revolt to Mother's protestations.

"Dashed landlubber" Father would call her.

"Not like us Captain," I replied.

My eleventh birthday came and went and I was parcelled on the train back home from boarding, and I was surprised to find Father on the platform waiting for me. He wasn't alone. Sissy was standing next to our nanny (to Sissy's visible disgruntlement). She was called Miss Allen and was a lovely young woman, though Sissy didn't think so. Both of them were kitted out in resplendent summer dresses. Father took me to one side and explained the whole wheeze. He'd been waiting for the opportunity to take Sissy and me out on a proper voyage.

"You'll need to work hard," he said as we pulled into the quay. "But you two are up to the task of keeping her in Bristol fashion."

He handed us both boxes wrapped in brown parcel paper. In Sissy's was a logbook; she would be quartermaster, in charge of the ship's diary. In my box was a cap with "First Mate" in gold lettering across the brim. For supper we ate fish and chips around the small table below deck.

At first light, we set sail. Sissy cracked out the log and dutifully wrote "For breakfast, toast and eggs." Afterwards I went up on deck and watched England slip below the horizon. We were making for the French fishing village of l'Escale in the Bay of Biscay. Father had once been there on a business trip. Our voyage was calm. Every hour of the day Sissy and I would spend above deck, sunlight tickling our skin. Occasionally Miss Allen would don her bathing suit to tan. Sissy seemed to take umbrage with this; when I quizzed her on her mood she gave me a dirty look.

"Idiot," she muttered.

Sissy's attitude towards Miss Allen was not new, but this was the first time I'd been in such close proximity to it. As tactless and oblivious as I was as a child, I could tell something was off.

This was not enough to ruin our holiday, and all too soon we caught sight of land. I'd never seen France before, and l'Escale was a wonderful ambassador for the country. The white walls of the houses made the whole village glow. We disembarked and walked to the cliffside for a picnic. Father and I wore matching striped shirts. Sissy wore a rather nice flowery number. Miss Allen had, at Father's request, purchased some sandals to accessorise her bathing suit. The locals spoke rather better English than Father spoke French so we were able to make good conversation with them. As I recall we were coming back from the market when we encountered a high-spirited florist with a rather astonishing moustache.

"Monsieur! A beautiful rose for your beautiful wife?" he barked at us.

Father had to stammer through an explanation that he and Miss Allen were not in fact, married. He bought her some flowers regardless. This event caused Sissy to take to our cabin in a sulk. Only after several hours of coaxing from Father would she leave.

The night after we left l'Escale I was unable to sleep. I was tucked up tight in bed feeling the pitch and yaw of the ship. The sound of Father's radio leaked through the ceiling, despite the fierce wind was battering at our hull. It must have been past midnight; it was playing the shipping forecast.

"Tyne, Dogger. Southeast 4 or 5. Occasional rain. Moderate."

I tried ignoring the wind and focused on the soothing BBC voice. Mother had told me she listened to the shipping forecast when she had trouble sleeping. I tried to untangle the shipman's code. Tyne, and Dogger were seas. Dogger, Fisher, German Bight and all that. The last word referred to the visibility. Everything else had something to do with the weather. So the report meant that on the seas of Tyne and Dogger, there was a fair bit of wind, rain, and fog.

"Biscay. Northeast 8 to severe gale 10. Heavy rain. Poor."

I became very aware of every scratch the wind was making against the hull. The door to our cabin shot open, causing Sissy to shriek. Father stood there, shirt unbuttoned, and soaking.

"We're heading into rough waters!" he bellowed at us. "Stay here. Do not come up on deck!"

And before either of us had a chance to open our mouths he slammed the door, and we were left listening to the storm. Sissy pulled her knees up to her chin. I felt calm. Somehow my hat had moved from my bedside table to my hands. I let my fingers pass over the engraving, "First Mate."

Before Sissy could stop me; before I could stop myself, I rammed the hat onto my head and ran out the door.

"Daddy said—!" was all I heard of Sissy's cry.

I stepped on deck in time to catch the first crack of lightning, and I don't need a picture to remember what I saw: Father, clothes soaked through, rope in hand, lashing himself to the helm. He saw me come out on deck, and called out to me. I don't know what he said, but I saw, lit by lightning, the fear in his eyes.

Water came barrelling over the sides of the boat. It hit me like an anvil, knocking me off my feet and rushing over my head. The floor was slipping away; I was being taken by the water. My hat washed off—*klang*—in time for my head to connect with the railing. Dazed, but I was thankful for something to hold onto. My mouth was full of seawater and my eyes were full of stars. By the time they'd both left I realised I was looking down over the side of the ship. I saw my hat float for a brief moment before being swallowed by the sea. I felt someone drag me back from the edge. It was Father. His arm was bleeding from where he'd pulled himself free from the rope.

He held me close, I think he was worried I would run off. I was in no temper to protest. As quick as he could he led me back below deck and left me in the care of Miss Allen.

I suppose I must have slept, though I don't remember doing so, because the thunder soon faded and we felt it was safe to make our way topside.. The dark skies were still churning, the weather's equivalent of a shaken fist. Father was slumped over the wheel. He was wet, both from the seawater, and from his bleeding arm. He allowed himself to be cut free before collapsing to the floor.

"We should get him below," said Miss Allen. "Sissy, help me."

The girls carried him downstairs and tucked him in. He'd earned some sleep. We drifted for a while. The storm had cut our sails to ribbons, and the galley was flooded with the water coming up to our shins; we were lucky to still be floating. The worst was over but the wind showed no sign of lessening and the waves maintained an assault on our hull. As the day went on the fog began to lift. I was the first to see the ship.

"Portside!"

There it was, a dark silhouette through the mist. Our rescuers. Sissy had taped a pamphlet of signals in the front of the log. I gave Miss Allen our flashlight and dictated the code to her. Dot-dot-dot-dash: I require assistance. They signalled back that they were sending a lifeboat. In swift time, Sissy, Miss Allen, Father, and myself were taken aboard the *Lux*. With the rock of a new boat under me, and the shouts of the gruff French sailors, and the hot chocolate they pressed into our hands, everything felt a lot more real now than it had at the time. I realised what could have gone wrong. How much we could have lost. I think Father realised too. Normally a jovial soul at sea, he didn't say a word to anyone until we were within sight of land, and even then it was merely a question of where to locate the restroom.

When we arrived at port we were astounded to see a great number of people lined up on the quay, many of them reporters. Cameras flashed as we disembarked, Father had to answer a great number of questions, over and over again, recounting the details of the escapade. He seemed to be regaining some of his old mood. Until the crowd parted, and Mother walked out.

Mother never caused a scene. She waited for the reporters to leave, and thanked the men from the Lux. They doffed their caps, leaving us in her care.

"I've booked us a hotel." She said. Ice ages passed in the silence that followed. She kissed father on the cheek. "Welcome back, George." Neither of them smiled. She did not look at Miss Allen.

None of us said anything on the way to the hotel. None of us said anything as we made our way upstairs, or when we were tucked into bed. Sissy seemed to roll over and fall asleep almost instantly, but I couldn't sleep. The silence from my parent's room was keeping me awake.

Eventually, I heard shuffling. The rustle of pyjamas being put on. The clink of the bedsprings and...

"They could have *died* George. Not so much as a note on the fridge. They could have died and I'd be sitting at home knowing nothing."

He didn't say anything.

"You are never seeing that woman again."

My parents never divorced. I don't think either of them were happy; one didn't get married for happiness in those days. We never saw Miss Allen again, and Father took to spending more time at the office than was his usual custom. Eventually he returned home, and life went back to normal. Mother's wishes bore out though, he never went back to the sea. On the one occasion we did go on a beach outing I caught him looking out over the water at the sun, settling behind the horizon. And that night, over dinner, he shared his stories with us.

Photobook
Ben'J Jordan

Peek-a-booing in cloud—
soft curtains. Crouched behind the sofa. Stolen
behind white glossed wood peeking in at all the big noisy
shadows across the ceiling;
beer sweat, smokey croak—
laughs, faces for names
the neighbourhood feared. Blowing
birthday candles dressed
up as Peter Pan and Playing Playstation not
talking to the other kids but
being sad when they left.
Catching the swish of whitepeach
blur in my peripheral mid-turn before I hear the
smack. Turning round. Mum
spilled on the floor. Dad's dilated heaving presence. Bouncing
off the nose-bleed-red settee and raising a tiny fist to squeak
'Pick on someone your own size' the day Dad left. Hiding
round the corner listening in to kitchen-table-talks: those after—
midnights he came back
to fuck Mum again. Holding the dragon
drawing I wouldn't give him that time
I showed him and he asked.

Hugo Simberg, The Garden of Death, 1896

Erin Ketteridge

We the damned,
tend heavenly garden with gentle hand.

The desert of the garden is far from the boy's bedroom, and yet Death can still hear him. Carried over the winds of hundreds, perhaps thousands of years, are the sobbing calls of grief that prove a loss
has been felt.
The winds rattle and wail on. They whip and they stroke. Sometimes they are warm and sometimes they are cold. Always, the Gardeners are unphased.

Death slows his bony-fingered work. While pruning the youngest nursling, he stops the chatter of his bones to listen to the child's question. The child asks
Where his grandpa is?
And Death clutches the forget-me-nots he holds to his chest. Somewhere in that deep cavity used to be something like a heart that knew loss, too. If it could, it would ache for the child, it would break for the child. He looks to the other workbenches, other Deaths working in quiet contentment in their shrouds. They are all white heads, smooth stones bent and eyes empty and gaping. They are mouths stretched in constant smile and constant grief. Constant love for this garden that they tend.

Death places the forget-me-nots back in their square pot on the workbench. With keeling, dry fingers, he presses the roots back in and covers them with soil. Death downs his tools and begins to walk.

Death walks for a long time. He walks through the wind-stretched desert, the silent storms that reign this place of purgatory. He walks past the old, gnarled trees that bear the only fruit Death can eat. It's dry and stringy, it gets caught in the teeth if you have them left and often pulls out the ones that remain.

Death passes the red flowers that bloom in the naked grass. He smiles at them as he passes, and they do not wilt as you might imagine they would. They beam back at him. These flowers are the souls that decided to stay - they love Death and all the Deaths that came before him.

Death walks barefoot to the land of the living, because shoes don't fit a dead man's toes.

Death walks until he can walk no more, and then he arrives in
the little boy's bedroom.
The child is asleep.
Death does not know what year it is, or, perhaps, how long it has been since the boy has asked where his grandpa has gone. But still. A question has been asked, and the question shall be answered.

Death slips an old, bony hand into the fist of the young, fleshy one, and the boy rouses.

Come, says Death, I will show you where your grandpa is.

Death carries the boy back through the desert, for the boy is barefoot, and the desert is no place for a living child's toes. The boy pokes his fingers in Death's empty eye-sockets as he is carried. He giggles as he does, giggles at the clatter of bones beneath Death's shroud, giggles at the red flowers that beam at him as he passes.

With his head pressed against Death's chest, he might have heard a creaking beat in there. Imagined, but warm and hopeful all the same.

Death and the boy talk as they walk. The boy tells Death about the latest football scores, what his sister said the other day, and the painting he made at school. Death hopes that the boy can see him smile as he listens, but his skeletal teeth and cheeks face the wind and the words as they ever do.

'What is your name?'

The boy asks in his wondrous curiosity.

Death, Death says,

and he is pleased to see that the boy does not recoil in horror at the way Death does not move his mouth when he speaks.

After many more paces, they crest the hill that takes them to the garden. The boy looks over the expanse of sand and purgatory grass. He takes in the rows of work benches and raised beds, the plants and flowers of all different shapes and sizes and colours. He looks at the trees of barren fruit with such amazement in his eyes that Death, if he could, might cry. The boy says,

it's beautiful

with his wide eyes as audibly as if he had said it with words.

Death feels something stir in his ribs.

Pride. Joy.

Pride and joy.

The boy points to the figures wandering the beds in their shrouds.

'Who are they?' He asks.

They are Death, too. Says Death.

'How silly,' the boy says, 'for your mummy and daddy to have given you all the same name.'

That's a family. Death thinks. He thinks a bit more, and decides that they are, indeed, a family. A family of Gardeners. Certainly.

When they reach the benches, Death places the boy atop a bed. The boy watches as Death takes two large leaves from the box of waste of freshly pruned plants, and brings them towards him. They glow with slackening charm as the boy watches them, watches the way they catch the glittering, blistering sunlight. With gentle hands so as not to tickle, and with the magic of the dead in his crackling skull, Death fashions shoes for the boy. Green and fresh, tendrils of vines for laces.

The boy is delighted, and therefore so is Death.

Death sets the boy down on the sand and takes his hand.

Let's find your grandpa. He says.

The boy skips to keep up with Death's gasping, rhyming strides.

The other Deaths bend their heads in silent greeting to the child, and continue with their work. The boy peaks up at the plants they tend to, fascinated, but barely tall enough to get his eyebrows to leaf-level. To solve this, he jumps as he walks beside Death, and takes in the residents of the glorious garden. Furry, fat leaves. Tall, gentle, white stalks. Fraying ribbons and dipping curls, bulging flowers and firm buds. Black straggly things, and bright yellow foxgloves. The boy will remember them all.

Death stops and lets go of the boy's hand, before scooping up, with perfect gentleness, the most bright white star of a flower next to the blue forget-me-nots. He holds the nursling in cupped hands, and brings it to the boy's eye-level.

Here is your grandpa. Death says.

The boy giggles.

'That's not my grandpa. He's much taller and rounder and louder.'

His body was, says Death, *but this is his soul.*

The boy touches a sparkling petal. He looks confused.

Death takes his hand, with the nursling now in the other, and they begin to walk again.

In the years to come, the boy would always remember sitting on the crest of the hill with Death, overlooking the sunset with the soul in his fist. He will always remember the kindness that Death showed him.

'But how is this my grandpa?' The boy asks.

Death sighs and is quiet for a while before he begins to talk.

When your body stops working, he says, *your heart and the universe begin to coalesce. Your head opens up, right down the middle, and from the inside something glows. It glows red and blue and purple and pink and white and all the colours you've ever felt. All of those memories and thoughts and feelings and sad things and happy things are like grains of sand. They are like grains of sand beneath the tongue of an oyster. They are all rolled together, and then popped out like a pearly seed.*

We plant the seed, and we love it, no matter who you were. We grow it until it will grow no more, and then we take it to the next place it needs to go.

The sun is a deep, hot red.

'Where does it go?' Asks the boy.

I don't know, says the skeleton. *I never got to go there, but I'm sure it's lovely.*

The boy will remember that Death looked sad beyond belief beneath all his bones as he said that.

Then Death sighed again and took the flower nursling from the boy's fist to cradle in his own worn bones.

In that parting touch with the soil, the boy said
goodbye
to his grandpa and
goodbye
to any fear he may ever have had.

When Death laid him down in his bed again that night at home, his pyjamas were desert dusty. He touched Death's bony cheek and said,

'I love you.'

And Death tucked him in with a swelling in his old, dry throat. A swelling that could never burst.

Years later, tending to that bright white flower, Death heard a call that was much hoarser than before. He answered it, of course, and found his old friend, the boy, now a man. An old man. An old man who embraced him as old friends do. And Death took the boy's now wrinkled palm, and led him back to the blooming garden.

He did not carry him and did not fashion him shoes as he had done all those sunsets ago. There was no point.

Death and Death walked as old friends to the cherished, blooming garden. Barefoot from the land of the living, because shoes don't fit a dead man's toes.

Vows
Erin Ketteridge

Golden bug, first love,
And lovers that run into ground.
Claw them up, freshly dug—
Back to Earthside, safe and sound.

Let shallow graves just hold bodies.
Not souls or soulmate's hearts—
From hillsides divine, and pine to pine,
'Til death us do part.

For lilting hearts, they wander on,
Far beyond the master's land.
No warning can turn a head in goodbye,
From devoted, adored man.

With hearts lovers bid bargain,
But which end could they keep?
Thoughts of smiling eyes, wedding ties,
May soothe them back to sleep.

Could there be more faithful acolyte
Than the newlywed who ebbs,
To take the hand, and kiss the feet,
To pounding of drumhead?

Open your chest, gaze proudly on,
What feasts in there, what beats in there,
What thickens and quickens,
Gives pieces spare.

Take only honeycomb,
From sweetest hand.
A marriage of equals,
By fools is planned.

And should you lose
What's not forgot—
Think not of cured limbs,
Or vows that rot.

Flip and twist, wish for lips to kiss,
Think of wings and setting sun.
Think of children, smaller hands,

All the lives that are yet begun.

Smile for love, Death and yours,
And all that it could be.
Smile for life, love to Death,
And Death in love, set free.

Salt Flats
Sebastian Lloyd

Tender tendon string, lined with sweat beads from hot
open palms, poring springs of hand weaving roots

Wrapping thumbs and fingers of warm bodies like woven silk in cotton sheets;
Salt flats-humid, course exterior

Paradigm shift; exception to a rule

His eyes in a crowd, like staring up at dancing clouds of
a million raindrops afraid to be a world of light

Hiding in strangers.

There, There
Chris Matthews

He was on a road.
This is a bathroom floor.
Won't find you until
the doctor calls on Thursday.
Didn't need to find him,
was a real event.

You just gave up
frail fuck, gave up
and smeared your drool
on the tiled floor.

Postman came to the door
but didn't pause to listen.
The parcel fell
and J saw it on the mat.
He saw, but left it for the doctor.

Tuna and Mangoes
Zoe Mitchell

Mummy didn't shower this morning.

That's weird, see: because Mummy always showers in the morning. The bathroom's right at the end of the hall—my end, just the other side of the wall from my bed. So I always know when she's in the shower. The moment she gets in, the wall comes alive with hisses and hums, hot, watery noises and Mummy's singing. It's Come On Eileen, usually. And then the water cuts off and the lock clicks open, and I know she's on her way. So I wait. It's the same every morning: she'll open my door, still singing that end bit of Come on Eileen, and scrub her hair dry. When she tousles it out, the whole room fills up with smells like wet and mango-shampoo. I usually pretend to be asleep, 'cause if I do that she'll stroke me awake. She does it at my forehead, round and round in little circles till I open my eyes. Her fingers are soft in the mornings—softer than they'll be all day—and sometimes little spots of hand-cream rub off in my eyebrows.

But today she didn't come. My feet curled as I waited, too hot under the duvet, and when I wriggled them my toes started hurting. I winced and pulled them apart. The nails had gotten too long, all curved out to the side like those curly swords pirates have. My fingernails were grown out too, but I chewed those short yesterday. I can't reach my foot with my teeth.

After a while—when I was pretty sure Mummy wasn't coming at all—I got out of bed by myself. It felt weird, going across the room with the blinds still shut, so I squeezed my eyes tight and ran for it. But even when I pulled the curtains back, the light didn't look the right colour. I sniffed, and couldn't even remember the smell of mangoes.

Mummy was in bed when I found her. The sheets were a funny shape—a little hump for her legs, caught up tight like an Egyptian lady wrapped in toilet-paper, and a bigger one for her tummy. The round of it arced out, swelled into the sheets like it was made to fit right there. She was bed-shaped and the bed was her-shaped. And when I sat on the end, the wrinkles flapped.

"Hey, sugar," she said, and patted the little empty spot of sheet beside her. I wriggled into it, curling my legs out across her bump till she winced.

"Back a little," she said. She rubbed my forehead as she said it, though, so I knew she wasn't cross.

But she was different all the same.

Her hair was dry and smelled of old spit, like bad-breath and pillows. And when I held her hand, there were cracks in it. I thought of Granddad's lips, the scaly look of them, rough like cornflakes in the splits. Mummy squeezed my hand, and I could almost feel the cornflakes at her knuckles.

"What's wrong, Mummy?" I asked, and her head darted. She looked dizzy behind the eyes.

"I'm just fine, poppet," she said.

But she got up before I could check she really was okay. The sheet pulled away from the bump, suckling at it and floating out like a parachute. I thought about this game we used to play, where the big kids would lift their arms up and slap a parachute out behind them, tucking us all inside so the middle ballooned out. 'Mushroom', they called it. Mummy's tummy was mushroom-shaped. It made me wonder if there might be a fat little stalk right inside her, beside the baby. Whenever I saw her tummy bare, it reminded me of mushrooms—their pale skin, the way it goes see-through if you cook them. Mummy's tummy looked like that in the bath, slick with bubbles that fluffed like a lamb's head.

"Let's get you breakfast," she said, and pulled her nightdress down till the mushroom was covered.

Mummy always makes me the same breakfasts—cereal with milk on weekdays, pancakes on weekends. She does them fresh when she's feeling good, and the kitchen fills up with smells like sugar and her mango shampoo. But mostly the pancakes come from a packet. Today's a Saturday, but she must have forgotten—she made me cereal, used the last of the milk on it too. I didn't argue, though, because the pancakes in the cupboard have gone kind of hard. Mummy usually has whatever I have for breakfast, but today she ate a can of tuna.

"Why have you got tuna for breakfast?" I asked, and she forked it into her mouth, greyish clot by greyish clot.

"The baby wants fish," she said.

I don't know why, but I liked thinking of that. The tuna looked gunky, all mashed up in the jar, but I could imagine it reanimated in Mummy's throat. It slipped together into one fishy form, ducked its head and dived down, rushing through her neck and flipping its silvery tail. Her tummy was full of fish and baby, and I could see them dancing together, swimming, making happy circles and bouncing, twirling—

Mummy clutched at her tummy. She doubled over, right across the table, and her face twisted up. The tuna can tumbled over.

"Don't worry," Mummy said. Then she ran to the bathroom. When she walks, she moves around the bump, so it looks like the whole of her is following its lead, letting it take control. When she runs, the bump doesn't wobble. But the rest of her does.

By the time I got to the bathroom, Mummy was on the floor, cradling the toilet bowl. It reminded me of the way she held me once, after I got lost in the supermarket. When she found me, she ran, scooped me up and clutched me into her chest, so hard it almost hurt. I couldn't decide if I wanted the hug to end.

Mummy arched her back and her neck, hair falling into the toilet-water so it was damp at last. But she wasn't sick. She just sat there, legs at funny angles like a Barbie's, heaving and making deep, ugly sounds in her throat. They were the sort of noises I know she'd have told me off for making. "Don't be silly," she'd've said. "That's a nasty noise."

"That's a nasty noise," I said. But when she laughed, it sounded all wrong.

"It is, isn't it?" Mummy said. Then she sat up on her floor. Toilet-water dripped down her shoulders. "I think I need to phone Granddad."

Mum never phones Grandad. He's always the one phoning her—every day, usually at dinnertime. Mum has this special eyeroll she does just for Grandad's dinnertime calls.

"You'd think he'd learn," she always says, and her cutlery makes a tutting sort of noise as she sets it down. "Now really isn't a good time."

But then Mummy was clicking her tongue, and I stopped thinking about Granddad and dinner. I looked down at her on the bathroom floor.

"Would you get my phone, poppet?" she asked. Then she twisted back round to the toilet.

I ran for her phone.

Granddad showed up twelve minutes later. I watched out the window for him the whole time. Normally, I'm not tall enough to see out the bathroom window—it's right up high, higher than I can reach by jumping—but the toilet is underneath. While Mummy was on the phone, I hooked my leg up onto the seat, and crawled across till I was on the tank. Mummy didn't even seem to notice.

"Yes, contractions," she said. "Yes, I'm damn well—"

And then she stopped. For some reason, she seemed to remember me, then. She looked up, staring me right in the face—which was pretty bad timing, because I'd just hopped up to the window-ledge.

But Mummy didn't tell me off. She just went right back to her phone.

"Please, Dad?" she said. "Someone needs to look after the kid."

And then she hung up. Even after that, she didn't seem to mind about me sitting on the window-ledge. She just vomited some more, heaving back till the toilet filled with tuna-coloured slush. I hopped down from the window to stroke her hair.

It was ten minutes after that that Granddad arrived.

He stepped into the bathroom, and for some reason he was laughing.

"My goodness, girl," he says. "What am I going to do with you, eh?"

But the thing was, he seemed to know exactly what to do. He helped Mummy up and led her down the stairs, stopping every time she groaned.

"Come on, love," he said.

Her bump rolled like it was nodding.

The two of them hobbled down, clutching at each other so hard I thought they might snap to pieces. Mum's fingers were tight on Granddad's arm—white tight, digging right in as she doubled over. She caught him in between the wrinkles, hoisting them together till they stretched pale. She's never held my arm like that. I wondered about her not-soft fingers, all her cornflakey skin crumbling up in his. And then I remembered the tuna in the toilet. Suddenly, the idea of leaving like that—of letting the tuna sit there, cooling, greying, sopping—made me want to shiver. I turned back to flush it properly.

The tuna was shiny when I got back. Little chunks of it skittered about at the top of the toilet-bowl, winking as they caught the sun. They floated like plastic bags in pondwater. I remembered something they taught us at school: about how mummy-birds feed the babies, vomiting the food so it's soft and warm to eat. And then I remembered what Mummy said at breakfast: "The baby wants fish". I frowned into the chunky grey toilet water, holding my nose to block out that sick, stomachy smell. Before I could decide whether to save the tuna, though, Granddad was by my side.

"Come on, poppet," he said. "Mummy's waiting. Better hurry."

"Is she okay?" I asked.

Granddad just squeezed my shoulder. "She's grand," he said.

"But she was—"

He pulled the flush before I could even say 'sick'. And when he winked at me,

I didn't understand.

The hospital floor was sticky like Blu-Tack. I liked the slow squish of it under my feet, the tender, peely suckle. Granddad tugged me along when I stopped to let it slurp.

"Don't dawdle," he said, even though Mum was going much slower than me. She walked with her head back and her bump out, inched forward like a sniffer dog's nose. When she groaned, it sounded more like a bear.

But then we were in the waiting room. All at once, there were nurses everywhere, hundreds of clean-smelling hands patting and pointing.

"Go sit over there with Grandpa, sweetheart," someone said.

I was about to correct her—say "he's called Granddad, actually"—but then another nurse pressed a colouring-book into my arms.

"Draw a pretty picture," he said.

And then they were taking Mummy away.

I dropped the colouring-book just like that. Crayons clunked against the ground, and the white pages flapped, rustling hissily like a goose shot from the sky. But I didn't care.

I ran to Mummy and threw my arms around her, bump and all. It was tight like a new balloon. She jumped for a moment – almost winced – but then she was smiling. When the nurses came to shoo me away, she flapped them off. I hid behind her bump.

"Hey, sugar," she said. She bent to kiss me on the forehead, squashing the bump up against her knees. "You alright?"

Her hair tickled at my nose. As I breathed in—as clots of it sucked up my nostril—I caught its scent; fresh like sweat and vomit.

And when I looked her in the eyes, I could dream I still smelled mango.

A Certain Cartesian Anxiety
Arcadia Molinas-Argimon

Once upon a time
I stood before a fertile easel
of a certain shade of clementine.

My chest was bare
his hair I held in fists,
and he pulled at the strings
of my frilled underwear.

I shared with him there
what I thought I held true:

that when time had wound around,
and left him tied and bound,
like a wise old olive tree
cracked and dry in summer heat,
he would always find me
devoutly reaping his seed
and whirring the machinery
to make him fragrant and thick
for a time long as eternity.

But what I once held tight, loosened and left
and I wondered where those words went,
the ones I had said about when, what, and then…

There were things around me,
like buildings and windows and bolts,
that didn't depend on me to stay or be.

I looked down to the drain at my feet
and thought of a dishrack when empty and clean.
It occurred to me that the line in-between
the gurgling sewer and washing machine,
was whatever I wished it to be, that is:
the world was what I wished to see.

To reveal another's heart
would require surgery,
so to mine I've laid siege
and forced it to see
that everything breathes;
memory, things; poetry.

112
Arcadia Molinas-Argimon

Two ravens soaring across Colorado sky,
make thunderous flap from their noble pursuit,
but together among mountains bear witness mute,
to the wretched woman writing sadly nearby.

She listens to music and her head thus occupies,
but to photography Tom Waits pays his tribute,
and reminded loosely of that once bitten fruit,
the wretch resumes her writing with this loving cry:

"Darling, I promise you to never stay frozen,
on the same page my eyes will not lock,
to even force myself if it is so chosen,

I will commit, just to hear new words spoken.
From ravens to frames, your ghost, he mocks,
dear, I read in your light and by you am woken."

Sterilisation
Farah Mostafa

I was born too whole to be wanted [1]

                                                          without space for anyone else [2]

and I couldn't exist before I could bleed [3]

                                                                        I want to be loved [4]

                but it sounds too much like violence [5]

---

[1] *and you would recognise her/ but for the tiled/ lines between you/ skin sinks into stained walls/ strange hands run/ over watermelon flesh, nails/ gouge out, crack/ open/ seeds fall to the floor—you don't/ dare pick them up*

[2] *the site of shame/ a body/ peeled back by/ incense and hurried/ grasps you hear/ like ancients you/ didn't think you/ were allowed to let/ anyone in/ substance trapped/ between shards of/ mirror you are held/ agape*

[3] *the devil's tongue/ is sterile and/ senseless/ so are you*

[4] *patched up with milk and Tylenol/ slab of meat by your bedside/ tactile deformation/ to be used when it's dead/ sewn up, putrid/ fleshed out/ upon your sheets*

[5] *and he/ searches for blood the way you/ long for something/ stolen.*

Safe
Farah Mostafa

our homes are safe. I think
of words like duvet. body.   heavy
like unbecoming. or stray enough
to be incidental.

waves of familiar static curl
as she steps into the room
to encase her breathing
replace her beating
with someone's broken
car light, misplaced path
of a sky-bound shot

see how she drags the world in
her stillness
fashions her skin to be softer
for the intrusion upon her

she steps into the room
strips the lining of a mother's
womb with a
eulogy left
to grow out of
bullet casing

Milk Dregs
Farah Mostafa

There's this word I can't regurgitate like
milk dregs I stomach because I was taught
to take without complaint and it should be
no different when he craves juvenile
wetness only feels dry cotton skin as
his fingertips probe the seams in between
the boundaries I haven't learned how to
clench shut. But he mistakes my silence for

pleasure, as though I want to feel his
breath on my skin like the gum that lodges
itself on the seat of a school bus and
his gaze that I couldn't outrun with his
fingers like ingrown hairs on wretched flesh
I never loved, now hate, no longer own.

Flash Fictions
Chiara Picchi

Effluvium
Tendrils of incense snake along the floor and up her body, moulding themselves to her curves, licking her skin with forked tongues. Wrists strain against the fumes, flailing, failing to loosen their hold. Flimsy fingers wrap around her throat and squeeze, lay their touch upon her lips, part them to slither down her trachea. She stutters, splutters, eyes widening as the coils cling to her windpipe. Alabaster skin turns cyanotic, stained purple by blossoming bruises. Arms slacken. Tendrils loosen.

Modern Art Installation
Entrails hang loose, dull grey made interesting by blood splatters – modern art spilling on the kitchen floor. Your flesh, my canvas; paint still fresh on the brush in my hand, its metal waiting to be cleaned.

Your limbs lie stiff: you're a mannequin for me to arrange as I please, your face contorted into Munch's scream, your eyes glassy, taxidermic.

You're my hunting trophy.

It didn't have to come to this.

You should have spilled your guts when I pleaded you to tell the truth.

Flash Fictions
Chiara Picchi

Living dead
Crack. I glance down. Hollow eyes meet mine. Feathers tremble in the breeze, extending upwards in a plea for freedom, bruised and battered where bone has snapped. I step back—ribs claw at my feet / penetrate fabric and rubber / flesh bubbles and boils / flashes white as maggots emerge. The pitter patter of critters crawls closer. Wiry legs latch on to jeans—the army advances, hungry for more. Mandibles sink in. I wrench my foot free.

Ubiquitous
Their eyes are everywhere. In the streets, in the corridors, in the walls …they never lose sight of you. When you sleep, when you work, when you watch TV, there is not a moment of your life where they don't watch you. If you go against them, they will know; if you comply to their will, they will know; if you don't follow their rules, they will know. To them, you're an open book. Your interests are filed: which TV shows you watch, which music you listen to, which sex position you prefer …nothing is secret. Every detail, every secret, every fact, everything is collected, organized, stored. You're a number, a number amongst millions of others…you're not unique, you're not individual …you're insignificant. You're nothing but a pawn in a chess game you have no say in. They'll use you, exploit you, sacrifice you for their cause …a greater cause they'll say…bullshit …their only cause is to dominate you, own you, strip you of your freedom.

They are ubiquitous, omnipresent. You can't escape them…not whilst your heart is still beating, not whilst you are still breathing. Run away and they'll catch you, oppose them and they'll break you, cave in and you'll be their puppet, an empty shell obeying commands like a dog obeys his master. No … there is only one solution, only one way in which freedom can be achieved.

My fingers are shaking as I write this—not from fear, nothing is more terrifying than life—but from excitement. You see …there is no greater satisfaction than knowing I've won, knowing that with all their schemes and plans they still couldn't own me. The noose is soft around my neck and I long to abandon myself to its embrace…long to find freedom. But before I kick this chair and leave you to your miserable excuse of a life, I needed to warn you. Your life is a lie, your reality nothing but a patchwork of illusions tailored by them. They own you. They always have and they always will—from the day you were born to the day you die.

Abych koupil rybu*
Jack Pletts
*(*So I Can Buy A Fish)*

"This one," I whisper, my words mist in the air, "it has to be this one."

I'm frozen in front of a small tub, eyes fixed on the fish inside. Steered by its fins, the great mass turns in one smooth motion. Its back catches the water's surface, presenting its scales to me, all olive and each glistening.

I look up from the tub and see Dominik at his stall on the street corner, bagging a carp for a girl about my age.

I refuse to leave the fish, fearing that it could catch another buyer's interest. Instead, I stare hard at Dominik, wary of the surrounding strangers, all peering into other tubs.

The girl eventually skips away from Dominik's stall, her bag sloshing with water after each step. Dominik wipes his brow with the back of his bare wrist, peeking out from the sleeve of his coat. He's wearing a pair of plastic gloves that drip water onto his apron.

His eyes meet mine and although his mouth is hidden by his large beard, the way the corners of his eyes wrinkle tells me that he's smiling.

Dominik walks over, excusing himself when he squeezes past a couple teasing some carp with their fingers.

"You're Tereza's kid, aren't you? Petr?" he says to me, "You must be here for a fish!'

I nod and point into the tub at my feet.

"You like my whale of the season, Mr Moby, do you?" he jabs a thumb into his chest and grins, "caught him myself."

"Moby..." I repeat. It feels right to finally be introduced.

"I have to warn you, he's a classy one. Might cost more than what maminka gave you."

I offer him a bronze note, but Dominik's expression isn't nearly as keen as I'd hoped.

"Petr, the whole of Praha wants this fish for Christmas dinner," he kneels down in front of me, "I can't just give him away for 200 koruna, it would be an insult to him. He'd spoil his own taste just to spite you—"

Dominik clamps his mouth shut, as if he's said too much. I don't know what Moby's taste has to do with anything, or why Praha wants to invite him to dinner, but that's not important right now.

"But máma wants a carp for Christmas!" I press.

"Is she here with you?" Dominik's blue eyes look past me, searching the crowd.

"She's having a bath," I blurt. He laughs and I feel my cheeks flush. I don't need máma all the time anymore. She might not know where I am or what I'm doing, but that's because it's a surprise.

"She said, if you don't take it, she'll come down here and shove it up your—"

"Woah," Dominik throws both his hands up, "message received, Mrs Svobodova. I'll get you a carp, just one in maminka's price range, alright?"

Dominik pockets máma's koruna and grabs a net leaning against another tub. He swirls the net around in the water, dipping in and out of a song, "Máma gave me koruna to buy a fish, I bought a whale instead!"

The other tub may be brimming with carp but they're all wrong. They're too short, or too thin, or too short and too thin. They'll swim right down the drain.

Every Christmas morning, I wake up and it's the same tragedy: another carp escaped down the drain. Máma always pretends she doesn't mind but I know she loves carp; she always insists on getting one. I can't let her be disappointed again.

"Here's one!" Dominik draws the net up from the depths and it's my cue.

I plunge both my arms into Moby's tub.

The winter air is bitter but inside the tub is worse. Still, my hands reach in and wrap around Moby's body. I lift him out and his tail thrashes against the water, spraying Dominik's back and another patron.

Dominik releases the net and its pole sinks into a haze of carp, "Petr! What're you doing?!"

His face twists and it makes me shiver harder than the water did.

I turn on my heels and bolt down the street.

I hold Moby tight against my chest, one hand on his head, the other cupping his golden belly. He's heavy, the heaviest thing I've ever held, but there's no greater weight than the dread in my chest at the thought of being caught.

"Petr, stop!" Dominik's voice bellows behind me, sprinting in pursuit.

I push through a group of men taking up the pavement, scattering them behind me. One of them calls me a word I have only ever heard máma use once; it makes my ears burn.

To avoid another similar incident, I slip between two Škodas parked on the curb, running out onto the road. Máma says cars have to stop if you go out in front of them. She also says to look twice before you step onto a road: "You never know what trouble you're about to get yourself into, Petr."

The men are shouting at Dominik now, saying all kinds of things that I don't want to hear again, like that he ought to teach his "son" some manners.

I run down the cobblestone road until I'm at an intersection with tram tracks. Apartment buildings loom over each corner, their pastel colours, so vibrant in the summer, are dulled by the grey expanse hanging over them. Trees, stripped by the season, line each street. Their branches reach up to prickle the sky.

It looks like everywhere I've just been and I'm afraid it also looks like everywhere I'm going to go.

I'm lost.

I look down at Moby and we're both gasping together, mouths open wide but while I'm drawing in lungfuls of air, he's choking on them.

I choose to run straight across the tram tracks and keep pressing forward. Just as I'm crossing the tracks, Moby thrashes his body. I try to seize his powerful tail but he struggles again and I lose my balance. Stumbling forward, I catch the toe of my trainer on one of the steel tracks and I'm sent spinning into the next lane.

I feel myself going down, face first, onto the road. I squeeze my eyes shut.

Something pulls me upright before I lose Moby and my front teeth, then catches me by the shoulders. I receive only a moment of relief before I'm spun around, face to face with Dominik.

"What do you think you're doing?! Do you understand the trouble you're in?"

he hisses between gasps, "I'm calling your ma—"

Dominik's head jerks to the left but his expression is veiled by the blur of fresh tears. I try to pull away so that he can't see me cry but suddenly, I'm flying backwards.

It's only when I hit the pavement that I realise that Dominik has shoved me. I stay there for a moment, on my back, staring into the sky; that empty winter canvas. Birds cross overhead, so far away that they're little more than rogue inkblots. It's not much of a sight but something tells me that I'm lucky to see it.

I wince when I sit up, still clutching Moby. I notice Dominik, now sitting on the other side of the lane. When he sees me moving, his shoulders slump with a sigh I can't hear.

I look at the road, expecting to see two black streaks running down it, leading to a vehicle. Instead, I follow nothing to find a horse-drawn carriage a few metres up ahead. One of its engines whinnies.

Two heads peer out of the carriage's windows. One of them sticks their phone out and it blinds me with a flash of light. They both start speaking to one another, but I can't understand what they're saying. I wonder how hard I hit my head.

From the front of the carriage, a woman in a uniform steps down. She's stiff and seething at us both. I can hear a quiver in her voice,

"What on earth are you doing in the road?"

"What are you doing?!" Dominik fires back.

They go back and forth, neither of them acknowledging the queue of traffic building up behind them.

Moby and I slink away from the scene when the woman talks about calling the police.

I see a street sign while I'm walking and wonder if "Dykova" is anywhere near my home. My attention returns to the pavement just in time to avoid my third collision of the day.

I jump when an Angel lets out a yelp.

"Oh, God!" she cries, stumbling back into the arms of the Devil.

I gawk at them. Even Moby's mouth hangs open.

"Gave me a fright," the Angel says, adjusting her halo, "coming around the corner with a thing like that!"

"Are you lost, little boy?" asks the Devil. He raises an arched brow at Moby but says nothing else. He doesn't need to because he must know. I know he must know. And I know I did wrong by taking Moby, but I didn't believe máma when she said that the Devil waits around every corner, and I never meant to nearly get Dominik trampled. I didn't mean to take money from máma's purse, and—

"Please, I'm sorry," I whimper, hugging Moby closer, who flaps his tail once in sympathy.

The Angel's frown softens, "Kid, it's fine, honestly."

She smooths her hair back, then winking, says, "we won't even tell St Nick."

"R-really?"

I hadn't even thought about St Nick, about the presents he would or wouldn't bring me, certainly not if he found out about all this.

The Angel shrugs, her wings rising and falling with her shoulders,

"Worse stuff has happened, right?"

"Yeah! I didn't mean to and I won't do it again."

"Sounds good to me," she looks at the Devil, "what about you?"

"No complaints here," he says, dipping his horned head in a nod.

I smile at the Angel but try not to look at the Devil. I don't want him to remember my face.

"Hey, we're out of sweets to hand out, so we're heading home. How about we give you a lift? Like, take you to your maminka or whoever?"

She pulls out a ring of keys from her robe and presses one, causing the lights on a nearby Volkswagen to blink.

I purse my lips, "Can Moby come too?"

My heart swells when the Volkswagen pulls into my street. I open the car door and the Angel slams on her breaks just before Moby and I are halfway out.

The journey was quick, I found a water bottle under a seat to pour over Moby while they spoke about someone called Andrej Babiš; I think he's friendly with the Devil.

I catch my neighbour, Mr Dvořák, on his way in and he's kind enough to hold the door open for me, even though he stares at Moby. We take the elevator together.

I cheer, carrying Moby over the threshold, into my apartment, then notice his shallow breathing. The puckering of his lips has slowed and mine begin to tremble.

There is only one place to go.

I run up the stairs. The carp is always meant to go in the bathtub, that's where máma always puts it. That's how it's done and so that's what I'll do.

When I push the door open, my máma's eyes bulge. One arm draws the bath's froth against her chest, the other reaches out to me. I see the urgency in her face and thought that she knew—that she knew Moby was going to die, that her outstretched hand reached for him.

I toss Moby to máma and before I realise what I've done, the momentum has already taken him from my hands.

Moby soars across the room and dives into the foot of máma's bath with asingle splash.

"Merry Christmas...maminka."

Máma stares and then máma shrieks. And shrieks. And shrieks.

Momentary
Jeanie Purslow

Film Photography
Thirty shots, the whole roll used,
The aperture captures our soft game;
we'll frame the ones we want to choose.

Some will have to be excused,
And some we proudly still proclaim;
Thirty shots, the whole roll used.

When love has largely been diffused,
Exhausted, lost its sacred claim;
We'll frame the ones we want to choose.

Outsiders fear that they'll intrude
The flash exhibits naked shame
Thirty shots, the whole roll used.

If gentle memories end up skewed
We can view what we became;
We'll frame the ones we want to choose.

These snapshots are to be imbued
With lust and loss and faith and blame
Thirty shots, the whole roll used
we'll frame the ones we want to choose.

Angelo
Caught him in the doorframe when the
midday drizzle kissed my forehead before
tiptoeing softer than the spirit into the kingdom.
That little white square on his black collar
beamed back at the ashen face of
the scholar and his smile was like
hands around a hot cuppa –
Our Father's porcelain warmth.

Without
It rumbles in these axles
and swims in my vision's corner.

But it sinks in the water
swirling behind the murk

breathing steady and slow
not going. Oh look

it's my daughter
and she can't be left in her cot all day.

False Conclusion
Layers of renaissance-painting never-ending stretching
layers and layers of ivory textures
flotations, fixtures, impressive pictures and ashen edges
it stretches it stretches unending
ineffable sketches impressions of nebulas snowy sky hedges

Still get rejected.

A sharp, hot want to charge through forest, try life among trees
whose chivalrous arms might seal me in darkness,
my chamber of branches, though dancing alone, she still dances.
I'll fondly embrace my circumstances – after all

the light doesn't bathe me, it blanches

it blanches.

7 Cheap Things To ▇ Solve Life ▇

Rose Ramsden

3. ▇ infuser will help ▇ tea ▇ fall ▇ out ▇ your cup.
   Price: £1.79.

10. ▇ the perfect way to get ▇ out of your toothpaste.
    Price: £1.71.

14. A set ▇ mistakes.
    Price: £5.39 for a pack of three in black, blue, and red.

12. ▇ portable ▇ hanger to help you worry less about your purse.
    Price: £1.40 for the blossom-patterned ▇

23. ▇ thermometer will save you from ▇ disaster▇
    Price: £3.99.

17. ▇ makeup ▇ will help you fix those ▇ mistakes ▇
    Price: £8.39.

11. Some ▇ meaning ▇
    Price: £1.31.

Teeth
Rose Ramsden

There's a gap between my teeth,
A silver where the edges of enamel don't quite meet,
Canines covered by a yellow sheath.

There's a gap between my teeth.
Open wide: my lips form a wreath,
Revealing wet layers of pulp beneath.

There's a gap between my teeth.
She wraps metal around the bone then gives a tweak,
Blood blooming inside my cheek.

There's no longer a gap between my teeth.
It's over. But
Red still spills past my lips when I breathe.

The Wheelbarrow Cross
Cormac Rea

For Lyra McKee.

When he was young, Tadgh knew little of the form and shape of death, and how we acknowledged or ignored it. Wee Nina McKernan had never attended a wake when she was interred, unmarked, in the corner of her family plot; plunged back into the soaking black earth to which she was still a stranger. She was sixteen and loose change when they found her on the shore. At the time, most pinned her passing as accidental; a freak tragedy in which a blossoming young woman slipped over the shore wall and into the aggressive squall. They thought her slender arms incapable of sparring with the tide. This image stuck with Tadgh: the girl with whom he had enjoyed summer school, cutting cloth for tents, and ratcheting tensions between classmates, did not seem like she could misplace her unabated breath. The boy, at first, felt insulted. He was positive that no hand, even that of Nature itself, could have dragged her under the brine with such maleficent efficiency.

***

Tadgh's mother sent him off to the wake-house with a dusty bairín breac and a mass card as cargo. Old Bobby Roach had been the first to croak this winter, and his death marked the opening of the wake-houses for the season. Attendance was expected from Tadgh's family, and at seventeen he was now old enough to play the role of envoy. The town and country were there, pouring out condolences like the dregs of a pint. The townspeople seemed to peel from the comforts of home for only a divine, select set of occasions: birth, wake, and funeral. Mourners moved like a riptide, heaving in and out of the house in waves; leaving a foam of stiff white roses and wilting lilies resting as shore-stains on his beech coffin. It almost seemed that with Roach, a part of their livelihood had passed away: some cog now paused in the archaic, coal-fired machinery of their collective memory. Tadgh was troubled by this mindset. Roach was ancient; his death seemed less like a tragedy than an unwelcome affirmation of reality. There was a certain rationale to it. It wasn't like Nina. Her orbit was fractured, half-spent, and incomplete. There was neither pomp, nor ceremony, when she was buried. Her father was forced to sneak her body into the sanctified ground. Hessian conformed to her posture where a casket should have corrected it, and the wet earth made her face up. Tadgh was never afforded an opportunity to see her resting like Bobby, starched and powdered white as a porcelain doll. All because she had punched her own ticket. He marched up the lane towards the Roach homestead, navigating the stream of comers-and-goers; the damp, sodden, bark-chip path exhumed in his tracks. The lane was flanked by an orchard on both sides, a tunnel of apple and plum trees. In the evening's blustering swell their form was obedient, bending and whimpering to the corporal wind. He stood for a moment. He thought of the captive fruit, and how their sweetness would remain tacit for another few seasons. Some would fall prematurely; bruising and rotting in the quilt of leaves that mulched and made fertile the ground underfoot. It wasn't even their fault; we all watched them slip from the bough. Still, we complained about wasting all that gritty flesh, chastising ourselves, and wishing to have celebrated it more.

At the top of the lane, Tadgh paused once more; this time to catch his breath. He squinted, hoping his eyes would catch a sliver of a familiar face. He was disappointed when he saw none of interest. Reams passed through the exposed seams of house: stitching themselves to alcoves and corners. Mrs. Roach, the widow seamstress, wandered wistfully along the front porch, crocheting with hand and needle the fine fabric of conversation. Tadgh gently approached, hoping that his ambassadorial mission could be carried out stealthily, that he could slip in for just long enough to deposit the mass card. His fortune stalled once more, as Mrs. Roach beamed at him through her damp shawl, deposits of mascara clinging to her veil. She immediately took off towards him, untying her pious hands from their set holy formation. "Master Dinsmore, thank you so much for coming out. Your parents have certainly raised a fine young man. Handsome, to boot!", she wheezed.

She was still smiling at Tadgh who, for a second, was puzzled by her tonality. He had initially thought her bombsite visage a watercolor painted by tears, not the rain and chiding wind. Indeed, Mrs. Roach herself seemed to be at the point of acceptance.

"My condolences Mrs. Roach; it's an awful tragedy. I remember him working in Havern's when I was a sprog, like. He was class, pure class—an absolute gentleman—"

She stooped over him to embrace; her posture crooked. Tadgh could hear the scraping of bones and the wheezing of dusty joints. He was instantly acquainted with the trials that age set her body's every slight action: the afterthought of youthful breath seemed a chore to her. She slowly reset herself from Tadgh's torso and stood halfway up.

"Now, now; these things happen, so they do. All for a reason. He's up there with our Seamus and Caoilte now, laughing at us miserable sods."

Tadgh nodded and wore the suggestion of a smile. He held his hands out, offering the mass card and bairín breac, to which Mrs. Roach seemed overwhelmed, and almost delighted.

"God bless her wee heart! Your mum shouldn't have. Take yourself on in there and leave them in the kitchen, like a good lad. Thank you so much."

Tadgh nodded and followed his marching orders. The kitchen was just to the right after the front door, which opened into a parlor. Bobby's body took pride of place in the center of the room: a Child of Prague was cornered by burning myrrh and consecrated candles at the foot of his coffin. Tadgh drew a cross in the air in front of his forehead, whispering a Hail Mary. He had no desire to hold Bobby's cold hands, so he headed straight for the kitchen. He heaved though the mass of bodies pressed wall-to-wall towards the open alcove that morphed into kitchen. The table inside was proudly adorned with mass cards, like a mantlepiece decorated with trophies and plaques. Tadgh set his pieces down and drew a long breath. He'd shown his face, and as that was all attending a wake essentially required, he could now execute his exit strategy. He headed for the back door; if he slipped out here, he could walk the long way home over the fields and have a smoke before he got back. His hand clasped the door handle, primed to twist. Suddenly, the packed bodies tore apart to reveal Nina's father, Mr McKernan, throwing his ring finger against the torso of Canon Magee like a punch. He was blind drunk; swaying uncontrollably and barking whiskey words at the priest's face.

"You're fucking full of it! What fucking God wouldn't take my child in? Is she damned? Is she?", he screeched.

Canon Magee wore an expression caught between fury and embarrassment. He pushed Mr. McKernan back towards the kitchen door, where he was grabbed by Bobby's son John, whose apparent impartiality spoke volumes of his patience and amicable nature.

"Mr McKernan, you're drunk. For the love of all that's holy show some respect. A man has died—"

"Get out of my fucking face.", retorted Mr. McKernan, jostling himself free from poor John's protective clutches.

"You're a fucking joke, Canon. My wee girl's as dead as Bobby. Cunts like you are the reason she did what she did, and you still have the gall to tell me she's unworthy of a graveyard. Not a drop of fucking empathy in ye!"

Each head focused on Bobby's resting form splintered, attempting to withhold from view the slip of their interested eyes towards the argument. It was only recently made public that Nina's death was neither natural nor murder. She had thrown herself into the sea. Canon Magee, ever the Papal loyalist, refused to bury her on account of Catholic catechism. They didn't even wake the body. The two men furiously continued to exchange words as Tadgh slipped out the back door. He needed that smoke more than ever.

***

Light slipped out of the kitchen but only kissed the verges of the garden. The rainclouds had broken, so the moonlight poured through their retreating ranks and half-lit the grass. Tadgh snuck along the back of the house, slipping out to the left where he would be relatively obscured from any prying eyes. A bench lay ahead of him, and in front of it a shucked ebony skull, forgotten in the maelstrom of mourners; friends longstanding and fair-weather alike. Time harried its jaw and cheek bones into the terse terra, making esoteric its pronounced, identifying features. Tadgh ogled the spent skull, its curved hollows protruding in his mind's eye. He thought, then, of his own eyes and their sullen droop, and the smooth sockets that housed them. This anatomical view was clearly alarming to him. When stripped of the biological certainty of pupil and retina they seemed so callous, inorganic. Tadgh's head stooped slightly, as he hunched to light a cigarette. He thought again of Nina, and how her amber eyes would fade when the soil finally reclaimed them.

Tadgh looked back to the house after every drag, cautious of a family friend glimpsing and catching him in the act. Stepping out, he saw a man half-lit by the kitchen lamp, his alabaster complexion betraying his features in the hard, white light. The man staggered towards Tadgh, unabated by the wind, with a hunchback Woodbine clutched between his haylage teeth. Anticipating the figure's arrival, he looked down and scrunched up his cigarette and stuffed it in his shirt pocket; painting his red thumb black with ash.

"Did you ever hear tell, young man, of the Wheelbarrow Cross?" the manwhispered, standing now behind Tadgh.

Tadgh spun his head around to examine the voice behind him. It was Mr McKernan. The stench of alcohol was pungent, but he seemed slightly moresober than when Tadgh had last seen him. Tears were sauntering down his face, as regular as rain.

"No, sir. Unfortunately, I've never heard tell of it." Tadgh replied, quietly. Mr. McKernan cut a sorry sight in this state, and Tadgh could feel nothing but pity. He knew Nina, and was mourning in his own right, but Mr. McKernan's grief was so much more.

"Ach, it was back in the auld days, when there was no tell of cars. A fella's mother said in her will that she was to be buried in a wee village thirty or forty miles away from theirs. She dies, and he takes it upon himself to do it. He hadn't a pot to piss in, and the neighbors wouldn't lend him horse nor trap. So, he wrapped her in a sack and stuck her in a wheelbarrow—honest to God—and marched her to this village in the pissing rain. A day or two later, he arrives. Now, as I say, he's not a shilling to his name. Not a penny. Anyway, he buries her in the family plot in the dead of the night. So, says he, I haven't so much as wood for a cross. So, he breaks the wheelbarrow down with his bare hands, and makes one. A wheelbarrow cross."

The tears became still on his cheeks, and Tadgh felt like embracing him as he had Mrs. Roach. Mr McKernan's eyes wistfully locked with the half-buried skull as silence overcame the pair. The shape of death revealed itself there to Tadgh, but he still couldn't comprehend its form: it was as deep and winding as the roots which now cradled Nina, in her forbidden resting place.

Plath's First Cut
Julia Reynolds

What a thrill—
My thumb instead of an onion.
The top quite gone
Except for a sort of hinge   *Sylvia Plath*

Dark fingers in darker hair,
Gripping, grabbing, groping the scalp,
Thumb stroking my cheek you kissed me.
What a thrill—

I stare into my crumbling skin,
Whorls and spirals of flesh and nerves and pus,
Sandwiched layers of blood, potassium, sodium,
Of red and white, pink and blue.
Spirals of DNA, adenine, thymine, cystesine, guanine,
My thumbprint and chemicals were falling away,
Layer by layer,
My thumb instead of an onion.

Inching to the end of the bed
You watched me adjust arms and legs, jacket and jeans coming off.
I plunged into your gaze,
Glazing my heart over and anticipating the cold air on red chest,
The top quite gone.

Hooks from each side of the wound digging in,
I tried pushing the skin back together.
Flesh falling away and blood cells evacuating my body,
The empire of my body had been conquered, no skin left
Except for a sort of hinge.

Baby Got Basiphobia
Saskia Reynolds

Mum holds my hand in the car. It's nice to feel the warmth of her skin; her palms are calloused from a lifetime of washing dishes. A lifetime of holding my hand, pulling me to my feet, cleaning cuts and scrapes.

'Are you excited?'

'Of course not. Amelia and Jas aren't even coming.'

'It'll be fun. More fun than you think.'

I turn to look out of the window. The Lake District's weather forecast offerssome comradeship; the sky is grey and sullen.

'Well, anyway,' she says, 'you look lovely.'

I know that kindness is expected from a mother to her child, but when she says that, I imagine unzipping this mound of flesh to reveal the grizzly truth within. Other times I think I was manufactured to be the ultimate test. God, or whoever, thought it would be funny to give Kindness Personified a run for her money, so they made me for her.

I'm wearing a bright orange dress; there's nowhere to hide.

'Thanks.' I squeeze her hand tighter. I am at war with my other hand, biting my fingernails until my mouth is full of tiny razors I wish I could spit out.

As we pull into a space in The Glenridding Hotel car park, I notice Josh and Alison sat in Josh's car, a few spaces along from us, making out in the backseat.

Jesus.

Mum laughs under her breath.

The hotel is old, red-brick, darkened by rainfall; a veteran of a better time. I wish I was a brick right now. Doing my job just by existing.

I'll bet the bricklayers would never have imagined their fine establishment being used for the Queen Elizabeth Grammar School's Leaver's Dance.

Siobhan Evans is walking up the path to the main entrance. Her short blonde hair hangs around her ears in elfish tufts. I still think about the time I caught her in the toilets–she hadn't locked the cubicle door–engrossed in a copy of The Iliad. She turned bright red and ran out of the room. That was the first time she ever acknowledged my existence.

She joins a growing circle of my peers; her fellow populars.

Alien thighs, alien thighs, alien thighs

I grab the fabric of my dress around my knees and hold it in my fists. Slimey. Mum would say 'slimey' with a grin and scrunch up her nose if she touched something like this in a clothing shop.

Go on, cry.

'I don't want to do it.'

Mum leans back in her seat. I follow the direction of her gaze; it's focused on the same group of classmates. Adam Wright's taken his jacket off and put it around Siobhan's shoulders.

When she's alone, Siobhan smiles at me in the hallway between classes. A smile isn't nothing. Something to show there's a conscious human being, somewhere beneath the lipstick and the indifference she shows everyone when her friends are looking. Then Amelia catches me staring and tells me to stop daydreaming.

Mum smiles at me, which is irritating, because I know whatever she's going to say is right. 'You just have to come out alive.' She squeezes my hand. 'And when you do you'll realise how little all of this matters. I get that you think you'd feel better if you could just stay in the car forever, but–sweetheart, if you did you'd just feel worse than you already do. I promise, once you get through those doors you'll realise how stupid it all is. Dare I say how fun. You deserve to celebrate all your hard work.'

'Mum.'

'Well, I think three As is pretty amazing.'

'It's fine.'

I wish I'd brought a cardigan. Something I could tug at, hide in, dissolve into.

She squeezes my hand again. 'You know, if anything starts to go wrong, just take some deep breaths and think 'carpe diem, losers!'

I let her think her words reassure me–really they just make her sound twenty years older than she actually is. I put my hand on the door handle. The inside of my throat has turned to lead; I feel it drop down all the way to my gut, saliva coagulating with stomach acid.

I open the door and move quickly enough that the door is shut before I take my next breath.

The air is cold; the hairs on my skin stand up, unified in the same thought: You're a leech. You think you'll survive away from her?

Just like a walking meditation on Headspace: one foot in front of the other, palms sweaty: don't touch anything, focus on your breathing, stop breathing so loudly, why aren't you calm? I can hear your heartbeat, that's not normal stop it. Stop it. Normal! Normal!

By the time my hands are numb with sweat, I'm stood where the others were. The ghost of their laughter lingers, drowning out the silence.

Mr. Hughes, the history teacher, is the first face I see inside. His corduroy blazer is camouflaged into the wall behind him. Sad beige. I'm envious. I try to wipe some sweat off on my dress.

'Hello, Eloise! Ready to have some fun, I hope.'

Creepy. He holds an arm out in the direction of another set of doors. There's a handwritten sign on them that reads 'Dance Party!'.

I give Mr. Hughes my best self-effacing smile before opening the door.

It's dark, which helps.

The door shuts behind me with a thud, which makes me feel like I'm in that film Panic Room, except there's no Jodie Foster, not even young Kristen Stewart and fuck I'm trapped—

Carpe diem carpe diem carpe diem.

Once my eyes adjust to the light, I see that the floor in front of me is not flat, not even floor. It's a staircase; a staircase wide enough that the bannisters aren't there to be held on to. They're just a practical joke. The girls walking past meall walk down the middle of the stairs in a line of perfect symmetry, towards thedance floor.

How could this be any less of a test?

Stop trying so hard.

Thirteen steps between me and—I shut my eyes.

I could go down on my bum. Maybe no one would see me.

Of course, Adam Wright choses that exact moment to look up. He gives me a passing glance as he scratches his nose. My cover is blown.

I want to sink into the ground.

The lump in my throat comes and steals the air in my lungs with nothing more than a sigh. Coward.

Shut up. You can do it, you can you can you can.

Pull your stomach in. Straighten your spine. Be what you should be. Be normal.

I look down again–Siobhan is smiling, still encircled by her minions.

I'd almost be happy to be as shallow as them in this moment, if it meant I could be down there, and not here.

Siobhan is swaying to the Taylor Swift song playing, and her dress, blue with little yellow flowers, moves like a superfluous extension of her body.

When you actually understand the words, when you're around eleven, cerebral palsy, they move around in your mouth like jelly; the jelly you eat at the birthday party of the girl who's captain of the netball team and has spoken toyou once when she told you to let her copy your maths homework, freak. When you say you have 'mobility issues', and the woman in charge of school photos looks at you, seemingly insulted by the fact that you aren't a quadrapalegic in a wheelchair. Freak.

What gives you the right to take up so much space? A staircase. Are you so special that you have to bring attention to yourself walking down the stairs?

What if the stairs were metal; metal like those contraptions they use for school photos, the headmistress turned to glare at me when I tripped three years ago, never mind the gash in my shin, metal that will cut into your flesh and you won't be able to handle the pain because you are weak, so weak, God, think of your poor mother, having to mourn over your mangled corpse—

No—

Calm.

Right foot, then left.

And then—

Everything is everywhere.

Bright orange,

Dull thud.

When the shoulder, elbow, wrist medley makes contact with the steps—I should have known I was never going to reach them any other way. My body does not belong to me. It belongs to staircases and podiums and climbing into rowingboats on Ullswater.

Look at what you have done.

I'm aware of the edge of a step running maligned beneath my spine. My head is hanging, halfway between two steps.

What a fucking winner you are.

I squint my eyes open. The light hurts—it's new. There's music. Whitney?

Someone's near me, standing by my left foot.

'Oh my god, Eloise! Are you alright?'

My body is too tired to do anything more than sag into the position it's already in. Siobhan is standing in front of me. Shimmery blue eyeshadow. How does she still look good from this angle?

Alien thighs alien thighs alien thighs

'I'm okay, just—' I move the words around my mouth, metallic with their newness, but I push them out. 'Let me get up, I don't need help.'

She moves back, like my words carry the power of God but, as I manage to realign myself and get into an upright position, I see that she just wanted an excuse to leave as quickly as she had come.

You are alone.

I stare down at my lap. The dress is fine. Not a single tear.

I get up, go back up the stairs, gripping the skirt of my dress in both hands, out past Mr. Hughes and back outside. I lean against one of the pillars by the entrance before sliding to the ground.

Josh and Alison stare at me from where they're standing, leaning up against Josh's car, cigarettes hanging from their mouths.

I close my eyes.

'Oh, shit!' That's Alison. 'How wasted are you?'

I think about the pain in my right buttock developing into a glorious purple bruise. A massive, sexless bum-hickey.

I look up to see Alison still staring at me.

'What?'

She laughs again. 'You're gone!' She holds out her hand, holding a pack of cigarettes. 'Want one? Helps with recovery.'

I don't move. 'Yeah, okay.'

She comes out from behind the cars. Her dress is black, the skirt juts out like a gothic tutu at her hips. I think I can see her pants.

She sits down next to me. 'We don't talk a lot.'

'No.'

'I always thought you seemed cool.'

'I don't smoke.'

'First time for everything. Do you want to talk about it?' She passes me a cigarette and sets her lighter down between us.

'About what?'

'Why you decided to drink so much you can't stand?'

'I—'

'Hey, no judgement. We brought, like, three hip flasks. No one's surviving in there sober.'

I fiddle with the cigarette. 'I got really crap A-level results. Everyone celebrating made me feel shitty. Needed a drink.'

'Oh, shit.'

'If anyone was going to get three A-stars I would've expected it to be you.'

Josh had silently circled around to stand behind Alison.

'Yes, thank you, Josh. Very helpful when someone is literally crying in front of you.'

'Crying?' I reach up to touch my face.

'Oh, Eloise.' Alison takes a tissue out of her bag and starts dabbing at my cheeks. 'You didn't realise? Hey, A-levels mean nothing. You're a good person, that's all that matters.'

I inhale the smell of tobacco as she hugs me.

'Yeah, u—'
'We were gonna drive to Ullswater to look at the sunset because we're old people. Do you want to come?'
'Are you kidding?'
She laughs. 'Of course not! Come on, it'll be fun. There have to be some advantages to living in the middle of nowhere.'
She takes my hand.
'Okay. Okay, sure. Let's go.'

Latte with Soya
Tom Rosser

He's got a big smile on. 'It's Nick.' he says.

'Oh, it's Nick,' I say. 'Hi Nick.' Train isn't due for three minutes yet. Delays.

For a moment we're just stood there. Then he points his finger at me, gunslinger-style, 'Basingstoke?'

'Basingstoke.' I say, looking away down the platform.

'I'm going to Basingstoke too. Business thing … ' He pauses so I can ask him what he does for a living. Once it's clear that I won't, he asks, 'You?'

None of your damn 'Business, Nick.' A flock of birds passes over the lines way off. Someone's walking on the tracks.

I'm telling Nick that I travel around the country to supervise the opening staff of new shops for an organisation he's probably heard of. I'm telling him that, although the job itself is very challenging, I like that I can go to see lots of new places. I'm telling him I have good friends all over the country. I'm telling him I'll be offered a promotion pretty soon but I'm going to turn it down so I can keep doing what I'm doing. And I'm trying to look at him as I'm telling him all this, but I can't, because although I'm talking to Nick, what I'm really doing is looking around.

There are security cameras all over the place and they're all looking at me. At me and Nick. At me and Nick and the girl with the pram and the baby both chewing with their mouths open. At me and all the rest of them with their conversations and their phones and their tiny make-up mirrors, looking at each other's shoes and tits and the fits of each other's jeans, admiring each other, ignoring each other, despising each other. And nothing, no-one, is looking at that far-off figure, too far to tell if man or woman, old or young, who's walking between the rails, tiptoeing over the sleepers, so nice and slowly, like walking in the park. Hands in pockets. No care in all the world. Nobody's doing anything.

'Linda is six. Mary is four in January.' Nick's pushing his open wallet under my nose, filling my nostrils with the smell of tobacco. His wife is stuck in there behind the clear plastic, tucked slightly behind the kids. They all look happy, but of course they do. I open my mouth to pass some polite comment but a bright Scottish lilt from the loudspeakers interrupts me, 'The train arriving at platform nine is the delayed thirteen-fifteen service to Basingstoke. Calling at Basingstoke only. Basingstoke only. Thank you.'

I leave Nick alone on the platform without a word and push into the coffee shop. I knock a guy with the door and he mumbles me an apology. It's packed inside. My head fills up with the noise of coffee machines grinding and Baristas hitting and banging things and the rolling thunder of chatter that fights to rise above it all. Someone's jabbing two fingers into the back of my shoulder, 'Don't you know what a queue is, mate?' I keep pushing, trying to get out of everyone's way, and I wind up somewhere pressed against a window. My breath fogs up the glass and, through the haze, I glimpse Nick and someone else running past, disappearing off somewhere out of sight up the platform.

The door clatters open again and again and chilly air rushes in as more people flash past my window. Space frees up around me. I can relax my shoulders. It's quiet inside. Outside, people are going, 'What happened?' Some people are saying, 'Oh my god,' but mostly people are all just going, 'What happened? Did you see?' What little I can glimpse of the crowd bulges backwards a bit as two women in puffed-up reflective jackets barge through, waving their arms and ushering people behind the yellow line. Some tall guy in one of those long navy coats puts his back to the window, blocking my view, speaking on the phone, 'I don't think I'll make it in today, Steve. There's been a problem with my train. A tragedy, in fact. Someone's been killed … My train, yeah, just now, as it was arriving … I did see it happen, yeah. Horrible … Alright, yeah, I will … I will, Steve. Thank you, Steve. Bye. Bye.' He dials another number. 'Hi baby, listen, I'm sorry about this morning. I didn't mean it. I'm not working today, so, let's something, something …

People are filing back inside, pecking at the shoulders of a teenage-looking guy with a rail uniform and a tablet and a head nodding up and down endlessly as he addresses question after question about alternate journeys and your other option and cancellations and death. Nick comes in, looking taller than before, supporting the arm of a scrunched-up old lady as she hobbles along clutching a trolley in front with her mouth hanging open and her lower jaw wobbling around. Hard to tell if she's devastated or just old. The coffee machines start back up and the Barista gets back to hitting that heavy handle thing against the bin and calling out coffees, 'Latte with soya?'

The train people know what to do so pretty soon I'm sat next to Nick on a packed rail replacement bus, rocking around, nestled in amidst the blaring grey noise of under-seat heaters and chatter. He keeps taking these big, quick breaths, like you do when you've over-eaten.

'I don't hate my job,' he's saying, 'but it doesn't fit, know what I mean? I'll stick at it for a few more years, but then I'll have to …' He goes quiet—just breaks off mid-sentence—scrapes his teeth over his thumbnail, starts chewing.

'All good, Nick?' I say, though I know what he's thinking about. He's still waiting for the delayed thirteen-fifteen.

'Lost my train of thought,' he says, 'Crazy day, right?'

Voices at the front of the bus get louder; an elderly man with the discoloured skin of a lifelong heavy smoker is going, 'It's selfish, it's plain fucking selfish.'

A woman sitting opposite him, with a baby on her knee and her hands covering its ears, says, 'Have some empathy, someone's, like, literally dead, and all you're fussed about is missing your train? Really.' The baby goes 'Blah, blah, blah!' and kicks its legs like it's trying to get rid of its shoes.

They go back and forth a bit, until it dies off and the old man shakes out his newspaper and goes back to reading up on yesterday's tragedies.

Nick asks me, 'What did you see?'

'What did I see?' … 'Oh, what did I see …'

'We were talking on the platform, then off you went … '

I'm telling him I looked at the tracks and I saw someone walking there, too far off to see much. I'm telling him I could see they had their hands in their pockets, and they were walking like they were walking in the park. I'm telling him people just don't walk like that these days. I'm asking him if he knows what I mean. I'm asking him if he could imagine walking like that with a train coming at him and then I'm answering it for him, you can't imagine it, I'm saying, and neither can I, I'm saying. I don't know why but I'm telling him that I think I'd give anything to walk like that for the rest of my life; no destination, just eternity to figure one out. And I'm telling him I can't understand why all the cameras point in and not out, why nobody looks out anymore and why we're all just walking round and round in circles and I'm trying to look at him as I'm telling him all this but I can't, because although I'm talking to Nick, what I'm really doing is looking around. I'm looking out the window, I'm looking at the traffic, I'm looking at how they're all walking, up to their necks in boots that hammer and thud and crack the pavement, tottering along on heels which home in at those cracks, passed over time and time again by shiny black dress shoes which are too narrow at the tip and rub and rub with every little tap-tappy step they take, and I'm hearing the footsteps trampling the engines of the traffic, clattering above the scratching chattering, closing in on us, fat, metal teeth, screeching—'What happened? —'Oh my god,'—'What did you see?'— 'Hi baby, listen,'—'Latte with Soya?'— '... plain fucking selfish.'— 'Really.'—'Blah, blah, blah!'—and all that's left in the aftermath is the rattle of applauding footsteps; a walking ovation.

Decade Number Two
Leo Schrey-Yeats

We build the past retrospectively. We will never outgrow the child, about six, seven or eight years old, dipping into the big box of Lego, cherry picking the nice, bright, colourful, funny looking pieces and shoving them onto the model in progress.

He reached for the last binder on the shelf and started flipping through the files it enclosed, skimming for anything that might have been important: invoices, contracts, signatures, anything with a name on it. This, much like the many binders he'd cleared through in the past week, was a treasure trove of memory, a collective memory belonging to the entire company. Three decades' worth of hand-shaking and signing, all compressed into brightly coloured plastic covers. He'd only contributed to the past seven years of the company's memory himself, yet it felt much shorter, as though there were events that were unaccounted for in his recollection.

He handed the box full of folders to a man in a grey jumpsuit, who grunted a "No problem" and strode out of the empty office. That was the last of it. As he was about to leave, he felt it might be appropriate to take a last glance of the office he'd spent the last seven years working in. To be nostalgic, right? In honour of the dawning fourth decade, the company was moving offices. It was not necessarily an upgrade, if anything there was slightly less floorspace and the women's toilets were rumoured to only have two cubicles. However, their CEO's unofficial "Fresh Start" initiative dictated that it would be for the good of everyone to begin the new decade in a new environment and "refresh the vibes". His eyes flicked around the grey walls and white desks, which now stood bare, spare for one coffee cup of anonymous origins. It was definitely... an office.

We don't know where we're going, we just know we have no choice but to go. It's been drilled into us; we're aimed at an unseen target and expected to throw ourselves at it. Much like the nine–year–old hurtling through a German forest, we surge forward, expecting that what or who we leave behind us will still be there. We are secure in the idea that if we were to turn around, they would still be following us.

He took the stairs back to the lobby. He didn't think about how this would be the last time he would hear the echoing footsteps on the hard linoleum. He was barely conscious of how many times he'd heard it before. He didn't notice the familiar feeling of the hem of his coat catching on each step, or the cold draft that pushed through his messy black hair as he stepped into the lobby. Something else he didn't notice was the person waiting in the lobby, until they called out to him.

'Marcus?'

He turned to look at them, still walking until he put a name to the face.

'Sarah?'

She smiled.

The smile merged with a hundred ghost images in his mind.

'It's been a while. Good to see you.'

They hugged.

'What are you doing here?' he asked.

'I heard this was the last day they were packing up the office, wanted to see it one last time. Thought I might catch you.'

'Thought?'

'Hoping, really.'

'I didn't think you'd care enough about the place to come all the way down. Since you—you know, quit and all.'

'Yeah well, I have some good memories from this place, as well as bad. It wasn't a bad few years.'

He closed his eyes, trying to place images on a timeline. 'How long was it?'

She tilted her head. 'I don't know, three years perhaps? Maybe four?'

It was five. He counted.

'I don't suppose you want to go for a coffee? Oh yeah, a hot chocolate for you, I remember!'

'Yeah, I'm free.'

One of the most fantastic lies we tell ourselves is that our memory is objective. We underestimate ourselves too much. We are far more capable of forgetting than we think—in fact, we don't even notice the strict conditioning we put ourselves through to shape even the simplest memories of our day-to-day lives into something tamer and more bearable. There's the boy, now eleven or twelve, who comes home from school already forgetting the day's trials. By next week he's forgotten his stress from the promises of Christmas exams, within a month he's forgotten how isolated he felt from his classmates, and at the end of the decade the entire picture is a golden blur.

It was a Starbucks they always used to go to. The benefit of living in the city was that no matter where you went, you were never too far from your regular haunts. It was closer to the university than the old office, but still within walking distance. They must have made the same walk countless times together. He sipped the hot chocolate he'd always had, while she had changed her usual order. This went unnoticed. The conversation was mostly dry and filler; complimentary inquiries of what they had done over the past couple of years, who they were seeing, she offered to set him up with a friend, he politely declined her offer. There was no core to their conversation, until he asked something that had been nagging him.

'Sarah?'

'Mh-hm?'

'You said you had good and bad memories from working there. I can remember plenty of good. What were some of the bad?'

She was surprised. 'Seriously? You don't remember the bullshit that happened there?'

'I'm struggling to think of anything,' he confessed, trying to dig deeper into the blur.

'Wow. That's… amazing really. I'm jealous actually. I could do without remembering that stress and shittiness.'

'What happened?' he asked, almost begging.

She looked him in the eyes. 'You really don't remember.'

He shook his head.

She sighed.

We're fresh from uni. Surely you remember that at least? We think it's a miracle that there's a company willing to take on two fresh graduates, even better that we're working together. We've just left the twenty-tens behind and we think it's our decade. But a company can really take advantage of young graduates; they're naïve, hoping to pay off their debt, in their first full-time work. We get the shit jobs, all of them. Our seniors unload paper after paper on us, make us deal with the most insignificant grunt work they can think of. You buckle first. There are tears. We talk a lot about it, and that seems to even out the stress between us. We continue feeding the beast, cramming all that we are into those big colourful binders. I wish I could do more to help you, but I'm facing my own problems as well. I must have told you about them. I'm certain I did.

'You remember that, right?'

He could not answer. He opened his mouth to say "yes" even while his mind churned, frantically clawing through golden hazes, trying to find her words. In the end, the utterance was stuck in his throat. There were no pictures to be put on the timeline, no ghosts. There were just gaps, craters that led to black speckling his memory—hidden under colourful plastic.

'Maybe you can remind me? I'm sure I do, I just forget sometimes—it drifts in and out of my head.'

She thought about it and even opened her mouth to reply. But like him, she became stuck. He watched as her eyes clouded. Where he had failed to find the memories, she lived them again. How long had she lived with them? Had she ever stopped?

'No,' she said eventually, 'I don't think I can.'

She quickly downed the rest of her drink and stood up. 'It was lovely seeing you again. I—'

'Sarah, I'm so sorry for bringing shit back up. I didn't want to make you upset.'

She smiled thinly. 'It's fine. It's good to think back on the past, especially this year.' She turned away.

Twenty-thirty. It still seemed distant, yet it was mere weeks away.

He remembered something. In the moment before she turned and walked away, he remembered something. Perhaps it was pure nostalgia, but he said it regardless.

'This will be our decade.'

She almost tripped over herself as she turned back to face him.

He linked his eyes with hers and repeated it.

'This will be it, Sarah.' She smiled again, the same full smile she'd had at the office lobby, the smile that shone like a beacon in his mind. 'Happy new year, Marcus,' she said. 'I hope you enjoy decade number four.' There is no concrete future. We cling to this abstract concept of "the future" as something that brings either change or consistency, although we can't decide which we want. We want to stay close to our friends, yet by next year we want to move to Switzerland. So how do we compromise? There's a young man sitting on a bench on campus. He's on his own, sitting and thinking. A young woman comes to join him.

'Hi there, are you alright?' she inquires.

The young man is startled. 'Yeah, I'm fine,' he replies hastily.

'You sure?' she asks, unconvinced. 'You seem a bit glum.'

'I'm just thinking my thoughts,' he reassures. 'I'm fine.'

She looks at him for a few moments without saying anything. And then:

'Your thoughts can think themselves a bit better if you say them aloud.'

He looks at her, confused. 'I hope you're not studying English.' She chuckles.

He's silent for a minute. She's patient. Then he says, 'I don't know what I'm going to do next. In the next decade I'm going to be in an entirely different place than I am now, and that fucking terrifies me. The last decade feels so close; I've lived it and I know how it ends. I just can't even begin to think about what happens next.'

She thinks for a second.

'Shit then. Sounds like a rough line of thought.'

'How would you rationalise it?'

'I'd just say to myself—"this is going to be my decade. So long decade number two—you've been good to me," and just get ready to take the punches as they come.' He says nothing, but he likes it.

'Now I'm gonna ask what I wanted to in the first place: want to go get a coffee?'

'Sure, but I don't really like coffee. Can I get something else?' She smiles. 'Yeah, what would you like?'

Before the First Date: You
Oliver Shrouder

I am obsessed
    with the concept of You,
not you (the singular)
      but   *You* (plural),
          the subject, the global,
          the   *You*
in every man that I can distil,
simmer to a warmth.

You   (*You*)   threaten to grow
between the palms of every hand I share,
    the spread of fingers with callused tips,
(putting on)   the rim of a shirt tightening over an arm,
        (you, paving-stone tough in an off-white tee)
(taking off)   the wrap of a muscle on a collarbone,
        (you, pressing out like a loaf in a pan)
or   the thrum of voice
dashing through gravel,
        (you, the crunch of a returning car)
every word weighted.

I see   *You* again, again,
smaller, but more potent,
in the warmth of an offer
        to make a coffee,
        (yours, Viennese, dark as your hair)
        to iron a shirt
        (yours, crumpled from being thrown off)
or in
        the pops of a keyboard, crafting a message,
        the juice of meat, cut from the gristle,
        the spilling of voices from phone to phone
and I can feel *You* getting closer,
rolling into a face, a singular you,
until you
        stamp me into voicemail
        that shakes like a sob against a bedside table,
        unheard over the shriek of alcohol
        as you scour another man's lips,
        waiting for me and my calls to give up.

At night
      I find   *You*   again, distant but again,
crouching like a fox at the end of my bed,
rusted with ashy boots, whining but
              never offering to get in,
           simply staring, head tilted left,
                        (wondering why my mouth
                        is fearfully glued shut)
waiting for its name to be called.

The Ages of Memory
Toby Skinner

From the Young
A blue bike that gleams in a June sunrise
With a rattling chain and blaring bell.
And Tetley tea beside toasted teacakes,
Whenever I felt unwell.
The sweet button eyes
From that stuffed rabbit,
Held when laughter turned to cries.
Plastic bricks and forts of sticks,
Heaps of leaves and amber skies.
Beach walks after picnics,
And action men that fought in wars.
Dressing up as doctors,
Never not odd-socks in drawers.
The splash of heat from Sunday fires,
With a crackled splutter of burning wood.
All I lovingly recall
From a lasting childhood.

To the Old
A comatose and dusty mind,
Meaning memories are hard to find.
As cobwebs cling to a greying brain,
Searching for a seat in a silent train
Of thought that has now departed,
Leaving you in lands uncharted.

Why is it so hard to see?
Past this shadowed wall of obscurity?
Where yesterday sits,
And last month checks the time;
What was my password for Amazon Prime?
It seems I'm holding up the queue;
Who am I sending this parcel to?
A forgetting fog firmly grips me;
Where did I last leave my car key?
My thoughts can't seem to take much more;
Does my pin end in number four?

Eyes glazed and physique weak,
A hollow skull sits on bones that creak.
Like a rotting fruit left in the sun,
Memories decompose of my grandson.

Cast in thick vapour,
A grey spray that sticks.
Causing thoughts to slowly sink
Out of sight as you forget,
As if my life has been reset.

Ladybirds
Lily Stirling

A ladybird trails across my sleeve, from inner elbow to wrist; red and black on primary blue. It pisses on my arm, or whatever makes that ladybird smell. I prod it with my finger, and it stops in its tracks, retracting its legs; a little ball of blood, a shell hiding from a monster fingertip, a giant ready to squidge at the word go. I decide to show it mercy, it continues its pilgrimage to the top of my hand, resting then bracing itself to fly as I bring it up to my eye to inspect it more closely. Its wings are like an old plastic bag; brown and delicate. Looks like it could disintegrate if I stroked it, which I don't. I don't really want to hurt it. I place it on my paper, and it looks like I've written a poem about a ladybird or something. It flies off and I'm left with just the smell of ladybird on my jumper.

It smells like geraniums in here, mind you, I suppose it smells like geraniums because it's filled with them. Some of them are a bit brown, I think I almost killed them over winter. I didn't water them enough, you see. But they still smell good, so I suppose they're alright. I reckon there's at least a hundred pots around me, they're all quite nice-looking, real-looking pots, you know? They're terracotta, pottery, feel dry and like chalk if you touch them, and if you were to get a cricket bat and go crazy in here, gosh would there be a clatter—the noise would deafen a baby! Obviously, I wouldn't do that, though, I don't want to destroy it, and I don't want to deafen a baby.

It's nice in here, I like the sun on my face. I like how all the plants look up to me, look behind me where the sun is floating.

I check my phone and I've got a missed call from DAD WORK. Everything jumps, we're all spooked from the next-door neighbour's cat. She's on the roof looking down at me, blue eyes in a big cloud of soft. She's pretty I guess but she looks like she's got the funk in her. She trails round and round and round and round looking in at me, but she can't find the goddamned door. I open it a bit and she sniffs through, peeking ith just one eye the colour of the sky or maybe the sea if you were in Australia or perhaps somewhere like Corfu. Her tail is brown and swishes and she looks pissed off, irritable but also like she wants to be friends but she never lets me touch her even if I wanted to be her friend—which I do, but I can't be her friend because she's got the funk in her. There's a water gun next to me, actually more of a water pistol and she eyes it up, all blue and daring and I hold it up. Put your hands up. She doesn't have hands, you fucking idiot. She's balancing on the fence, can't decide this side or that, I squirt, and she looks offended, fluffy and pretty and threatening, I do it again, she flips off backward into the sound of children squealing in fits of giggles. I didn't want to shoot her, but she doesn't live here, next door is her home.

DAD WORK is calling again. Everything in the greenhouse is dripping, dripdripdrip drip drip dripdripdrip. They're all quenched and I'm thirsty, and a boy is messaging me, asking if I wanna have sex. I've got white on my tonsils so I don't really fancy it, and anyway I'm fascinated by the bee, brown and yellowy, slamming against the glass over and over and buzzing like it can't get out. There's so many windows open now it could easily get out; I think it must be happy here otherwise it would have left by now. It's quite strange to hear the bee buzzing, it's humming and whirring in my ear like an earworm, but it sounds like spring and summer and I realise I haven't heard one since probably September. It stops and rests on my leg, I could crush it if I wanted to, stab my pen in it's heart. I save its life and brush it onto a flower. I don't want to hurt a honeybee.

A dog starts barking next door and I jump because the cat is on the fence again looking at me, gosh she's so pretty and I think I'm in love. The plants are still dripping and there's the incessant bee noise bashing against a glass, with some flies zooming round my head too. I've got another missed call from DAD WORK, so I keep on sitting here with my eyes shut. It's like I can almost feel the vitamin D from the sunshine. It feels nice on my eyelids, they have been looking pretty pale and it is kind to my eyes to rest like this. I'm so tired. The dog barks in time with the children who are playing with their dad next door. He's teaching them a game and it sounds like they're getting the hang of it. It's peculiar to think that this may be only their third or fourth spring as they are now. I reckon it feels fresh and yellow for them, like when you peel a poppy prematurely and it looks like a new-born baby. Another dog across the village huffs back at the one next door and pretty blue eyes is looking wacky in my snowdrops. The snowdrops look a bit worse for wear now, they aren't all clean snowfall but when it goes brown and icy. I hold my foot above one and I want to crush it but then I realise that it wouldn't feel like crushing a razor shell—my sister once got cut by a razor shell, so I always crush them as much as I can—but this snowdrop is delicate and lovely, so I think it's pointless, I don't want to damage something so lovely.

I can hear a song playing across the road and it sounds muffled and kind of like summer when it's really hot and you can hear people playing football at the playing fields, and hear the sound of lawn mowers and hoses spraying little sisters in the garden next-door but one. But this song doesn't really sound like anything, it sounds like winter and it reminds me of this boy that makes me feel all giddy, which is weird because I don't normally feel very giddy. Him and me always had a good laugh and always stayed out too late, but we're not really allowed to anymore. This song makes me feel sad to think we shouldn't talk, and so I go to text him, and I can see another missed call from DAD WORK, and then I remember that I shouldn't message this boy, because one doesn't crush a sunflower with a hammer.

There's more buzzing, then I realise it's my phone, not a bee or a fly, but DAD WORK. A door slamming over the road. I look at my phone gyrate on my lap, it looks uncomfortable, it looks ready to fall and smash on the concrete. I wouldn't let it fall, I have too many pictures of that boy on it, it would be sad to watch it fall. But DAD WORK is still calling, and it won't stop vibrating on my thigh. I look up and see him walking up the garden, phone to his ear. He's found me. Hello darling, you alright? Yeah, I'm good how are you. Yeah, I'm good, it's nice to see you darling, here've you been? I say I've been in the greenhouse, because that's where I have been. His voice sounds like liquor and smells like wine. Puffy cheeks, yellow eyes, you know the deal. When I used to go in the car with him, he would keep driving even if a rabbit was dazzled in headlights, and there were always pheasant feathers stuck in the grills on the front of his car. He's talking still, telling me about a new idea he's got for this job that he's going to get, and the cat next door is on the fence, deciding what to do, she looks funky still, funny and weird and dazzled. She looks all scared at the sound of my dad's voice. I wonder what it would be like to spray the water pistol at him instead of her, and I deliberate, trying to think why I shouldn't. He's a bit like a razor shell, he's not soft, and he's not a sunflower, he's not a snowdrop or a baby. I pick up the pistol and pull the trigger. I look down at myself and it looks like I'm covered in lots of little red ladybirds.

When the weatherman sleeps
Madu Udeh

Season: FLAVOUR

we pull quick
we slink even slower
we buy funeral plots in weather balloons

heed no more
for the weatherman sleeps

Season:GHEE

born track
untracked tracks

logo'd track
bitchin' tracks
tree track

lost track
found track
⅓ track

lost track
found track
dead tracks

smart tracks
saved tracks
fast tracked
fact tracked

retractable green umbrella, red coat, and crimson soled shoes
you gotta wai—

traaaaaaaaaaaaack

clinkity-click-clock
floors are slippery when encased so please just fucking pay

50 dollars for flying lessons

Season: FUBU LAND

I woke up in a white bronco.
I looked ahead and saw a kink in time.
and then the car went cu-cu-cu-cu.
so both me and Bernie Mac got out and started pushing th—
Wait did I tell you Bernie Mac was in the car? Ya Bernie Mac was driving me when I woke up sprawled out in the back of a white Bronco
and as my eyes drew focus—I seen another dimension curl in on itself and we was moving right towards—
and then I hear a noise: cucu - cucu - cucu
Bernie said Oh No. And then he got out the car and so I got out to help too. When I got out the car, I saw it was like 3-somethin' and I knew cuz the acrylic nails in the sky said so. And if we didn't get to pushin' we was gonna to be late to FUBU LAND and if—
Wait did I tell you we was going to FUBU LAND? Ya so we was going to FUBU LAND.
And on the way there I was sleep-sleep on this nice plush orange leather seats wrapped tight in a cheetah blanket. It took me a minute for my eyes to readjust to this world. I looked in the driver seat and I seen a black man driving me and he look a lot like Bernie Mac. That man turned around and showed me his name tag it said—Bernie Mac—and under it, it said—Welcomer of the Good People—and on top of it, it said FUBU LAND. I looked beyond the glass and in the distance I seen a bundle of black intertwined. As we got closer, Solange's voice on the stereo started to distort and slow down—all of a sudden I heard something deep in the belly of the car. The car went couuu-couuu-couuuuuuuuuu. And Solange's voice stopped. Bernie got out the car and he yelled at me "Boi if you don't" so I did and we started pushing. He told me the event started at dark so we needed to get going. I asked him who all gonna be there? And he started saying all these names of people I knew but never met and met but never knew. Then—I told you about the nails right? Well they started to chip. All of a sudden a black light went over the sky and the road went transparent—well it wasn't really a road. It was more like those floral curtains your grandma puts on and calls a dress. Anyway—yea, so all of a sudden the sky and everything else looked different—Bernie Mac was still there but his afro was Pink now. And all around us Neon forms crystalized. Going about their business buying pockets and okras, earthquakes and teeth from market stalls.
Wait did I tell you about the market stalls? Yea there was market stalls all up and down the slick street. So when I was looking out the window with my misty red eyes—I looked to the right first and saw those empty market stalls. I looked down and saw I had a mink fur coat on. I looked up and saw the gold path we was driving on, ended in about 500 meters. And at the end—I saw a black meadow of textured strands folding in on itself. I looked to the left and I saw a man in a striped black and white suit. Are you? I say aloud. No I ain't you daddy, now go back to sleep. He said. So I did.

Starlight
Megan Watts

It was a Danish boy, one summer's night,
Who taught me how to read the stars.

In a place so foreign, yet so familiar
(Adrift in travel as we were)
He cried:
Look south for Cassiopeia, that magic key—
Trail your eyes over the sideways W, the 3,
That faint shape gracing the tops of the trees and find
The North! Nestled in the curve of the bear cub's back—
All you have to do is *trace*
The edges of your plough,   my mother's saucepan,   our big dipper
Following the lines of starlight
Until they lead you to our next adventure.

(Many, many, *many* moons later)
Under a foreign, frosted sky
We stood as sentinels—upturned and beaming—
Revelling in the dark of night
Fumbling with the buckles of Orion's belt,
Following the lines of starlight
Until they lead us home.

Faces of Grief
Shi Yap

Quietly, in the corner of the hospital ward with his family around him, he drew his last breath. His right eye was cloudy and still slightly open. His mouth was ajar. It was his most peaceful face in the past few months. Death arrived, pitied his sad height, and mercifully ushered him away.

Just like that, his six-month long battle with cancer ended. He's free from suffering.

The nurses drew curtains around the bed for the crying family's privacy. Grief festered in the dimmed, isolated corner. His family did not understand why he—a son, a husband, a father – had to die at the age of 59; they did not understand why the pancreatic cancer had to relapse and cause him to suffer for six months. They tried rationalising: he isn't suffering anymore; at least he passed away painlessly; he died with no regrets—he has led a fulfilling life. Even so, human language cannot adequately express the grief that throbbed and trembled in the family's bodies.

The truth was that they were never ready for his death no matter how much they readied themselves. In their small actions, all of them clung desperately to his remaining, limited days.

This was how they grieved. This was how my family, including my father himself, grieved for his imminent, inevitable death.

*

This was how he grieved.

After one of the random bouts of extreme pain in his lower back, he begged the nurse to end it all. The doctor had already announced that he was going to pass away in one month, so why prolong it? The nurse shook her head; Singaporean law dictated him to continue living, to continue suffering.

"Why? Life is like a game. I need to die before I can restart my whole life again."

To him, games provided an easy source of entertainment throughout his life. Up till his hands went numb, he never stopped playing Candy Crush or watching tennis matches on his phone. In the throes of death, he confided in games to distract himself from any negative thoughts.

One week after his hospitalization, his older sister came down to the hospital to visit him. Just like him, she was an avid player of Candy Crush. They fiddled with their phones in silence, their fingers swiping left and right to arrange the candies into groups.

"Di," his sister said, "what level are you on now ah?"

"4098."

"Still haven't catch up? I'm already at level 4160 leh," she chuckled.

The corner of his lips tugged upwards. He had been competing with his sister in Candy Crush for the longest time and could never seem to overtake her. Yet, like every game, there would be a time where the game ends, where his fingers stop moving. He took comfort knowing that there would be a restarting point, that one day he would replay life again with a newer, healthier body.

"Aiya, I'm tired. Don't want to play anymore." He closed his eyes; under the morphine's constant drip, his eyelids felt heavier than ever. He lowered his hand and it sank comfortably into the mattress. Then he drifted off to sleep, lightly snoring.

This was how his wife grieved.

She took care of him like she would a baby. She would cut the hospital lunches and dinners into bite sized pieces and feed him. She would shave his beard with an electric razor. She would brush his teeth when he was woozy from the morphine. She would scratch his back when he complained that it itched. She obsessed about the little things and clung onto them because those were her only way of relieving her husband of any discomfort.

One night in the hospital, he snapped at her. "I don't want to brush my teeth already lah. What's the point? Let my teeth rot. Nothing matters anymore."

"Don't," she said. "Don't say that. You better let me brush your teeth, or else I will get angry."

He did not have the energy to argue with her. So he let her meticulously brush his teeth. She brushed away the pulps of orange and bits of chicken stuck in between the teeth, occasionally asking him to gargle and spit out the pulpy, yellow-greenish water. She berated him for not taking care of his dental health; as long as he was still alive, he had to take care of himself. But deep within her, she knew that his dirty mouth was a bleak reminder of his sickly condition; the tumour had travelled to his brain and affected his nerves, hence his numb mouth and tongue.

She relished in the routine because she was afraid of the change that would soon wrench her husband away into the dying of the light. She tried her best to go down every day and chat with him about everything, from their irretrievable pasts to a future where he would be gone, where she would become a widowed mother.

And every night before she left the hospital, she would insist on hearing him say goodbye. A soft, wispy bye.

*

This was how his mother grieved.

The night before he passed away, his body began to shut down like a corrupted computer system, and entered a near-comatose state. He could barely open his mouth to talk, his breath not strong enough to fog up the oxygen mask. So when the nurse called his family and told them to get ready, they knew it was time. His immediate family rushed down at 2.30 a.m. Everyone greeted his frail, almost unresponsive body with tears. Everyone but his mother. She came to his side, cradled his hand in hers, and made him hold onto two $50 bills. She told him:

"不要放开, 要☒☒握着." She believed that if he held onto the money, he would enter the afterlife with money to look after himself.

Money, to her, was a source of comfort, because she practised a religion where burning paper money was a form of reverence. Or perhaps it was the comfort in knowing that money will outlive her. After all, her parents, her husband, and most of her siblings had passed away; for the past thirty-odd years, she had to pay her respects to all of them during Qingming festival.

And now, her son was dying; she would soon have to pay respect to him as well. For the next twelve hours in the hospital, she didn't shed a tear. She stayed by his side throughout the night, making sure he didn't let go of the two $50 bills in his hands, never shedding a single tear. Maybe she had to appear strong in front of her children and grandchildren. Or maybe she had no more tears to shed after seeing her close ones pass away one by one, while she lived on.

But eventually, the cruel reality came. When her son drew his last breath, she, like everyone else, cried. The tears came fast, and she crumpled the dollar bills that fell out of her dead son's hands.

*

This is how his son grieves.

His attempts to write out his personal feelings turn out to be messy and frivolous. An excess of emotions threaten to undam themselves in his writing. He fails to pen down this excess. He flails like a fish above water, unable to breathe even with the surplus of oxygen.

But he wants to bear witness to the faces of grief in his family. More than anything, he wants to pay tribute to his father who never voices his love with words, but shows it through small, accumulated actions. So he distances himself from the page and sees himself and everyone else. Then he writes. He cries as he writes, and he doesn't stop. Because that is his only way of showing how much he misses him.

Perhaps in the future when he looks back, he will have accepted his father's death as an inevitable occurrence. But until then…

**

Three days after the pronouncement of Pa's death, he was cremated. Everyone cried as he was sent off for cremation. The worst was over. The next morning, my family, consisting of my grandmother, mother, sister and I, and my uncle went to collect his bones and ashes from the crematorium.

Ma said with a vengeance that the cremation ought to have destroyed every cancer cell. As she spoke those words, a monk asked each of us to place a piece of his brittle, ashy bone into a white, porcelain urn. It's a Buddhist ritual: the immediate family has to pick a piece of the bone and place it into the urn, so that his spirit will move to a new house.

"Your father has really healthy bones," the monk said while he sorted out the bones.

"Ya, he was a tennis player last time," Ma said. "But what's the use? In the end, the cancer cells took him away."

As the son of the family, I was tasked to carry the urn. It looked deceptively light, yet it weighed down my embrace. We followed the monk to the columbarium, my father's final resting place. The spiciness of the burning joss sticks had become a familiar smell, clinging onto me like a set of clothes worn for consecutive days. The sound of the wooden fish echoed in the high-ceiling temple, accompanied by the monk's bright voice as he sang out the rites. We walked down a sheltered walkway to the columbarium, the walls carved with patterns of lotuses and deities.

"你要跟爸爸図:搬家了, 爸爸," Grandma told me while we walked. When she said that, I couldn't help but imagine how our home wouldn't have Pa anymore; how Pa would no longer be sitting on the sofa playing Candy Crush, no longer be cooking his garlicky aglio olio for our family, no longer be coming back home with his huge sports bag slung over his shoulder. He was no longer here. I looked down at the urn and said:

"爸, 搬家了."

---

[6] *Translation: Don't let go, you must hold onto [the money] tightly.*
[7] *Translation: "You should tell your father: we are moving you to a new house, Father."*
[8] *Translation: "Father, we are moving you to a new house."*

Cleansing Shallows
Katherine Yong Yhap

"Tday tha wind wus fullo meat. Burnin burnin all night froo. Mister come, fullo soot said thees ones juicy, lived in tha orhards three orcles of appleaters thay brough to tha pit. Full as an egg now, meh an tha babba.

 I cn hear waters all round. Whoosh an gurgle by edrippy walls round an knobby like muh tum. Missus says Ill quickin soon, babball be outo meh an cryin shittin like Mister. They were swellin an gaspin in eachuther when I rested fullo appleaters. Missus wants a big belly too, but Mister said thay no do it for babba, Missus too ole. Want some?"

 Greg grinned, shook his head at the proffered chunk of burnt meat. He knew by now the apple eaters walked on two legs, not four. His job was to observe, record and return.

 Whilst mapping the ever-changing Eastern flats, Greg had come across Mister paddling his abattoir of a coracle about the highlands of Grimes Graves. Following a frenzied, inarticulate shower of threats, Mister's interest in Greg's smooth oars, peculiar clothes and more: the food in his sack, had led to some cordiality. Now, after months of silent barter, he was permitted to enter the pits to listen to Ella sister-wife and Missus mother-wife.

 Ella peered at him through close set, pale blue eyes. "What you brought us?"

 Smiling again, Greg reached into his sack and pulled out a large fired bowl. Glazed on the inside, it rounded like the swell of Ella's belly. "Slike Toms barrel. Noras pretty but…" She traced the rough outer with grimy fingers, then it's glossy, smooth inner. Rocking on her haunches, she was silent. They sat like that for some time. Greg stood to leave; Ella made no sign of farewell. This man had come into her shaft of a world, and she had no fear of him, or anything or one else. He turned and placed, one on one, apples, plums and a couple of rough, seeded loaves into the bowl. Ella reached in and began the serious work of devouring all before the returns of Mister and Missus.

***

Greg set off on his ritual cursus through the chimneys of cobbles and chalk. On a series of spindly ladders propped firmly in scansorial ascent, he rose through the earth where no time at all had passed since the bipeds known as people first came to this place, forever ago.

***

Upon reaching the height of incongruous metal struts, Greg paused and pulled from his thigh pocket a slim hollow of matte metal tubing. Flipping the ends into right-angles he held one against his eye, and slowly turned in a full revolution. Satisfied, he pulled himself over the final few feet into the tumbledown building which hunkered across the pit's opening.

 In this space he paused and took a draught from the skin looped to his waist. The leather imparted a staleness to the water, wrinkling his nose, but it was clean and it refreshed him.

  Checking every aperture before leaving the hut, he moved outside to his coracle which lay like a heifer on the meadow of the island. Pulling the oars from his sack, he flipped the craft and slid it into the water, catching the tide surging West.

***

The city of Peterborough rose hugely from the wash, distant still and heartbreakingly beautiful with the water full tide high, a mirror without a ripple. The bones of the old world temporarily submerged beneath teeming flocks of waterfowl on islands made rich with their guano; Greg sought the secret paths between the-sandbanks to the port of Ely.

The sails of fishing wherries glowed white in the moonlight and golden from the harbour lamps, marking a colour-coded path to shore. His dripping coracle deposited near the harbourmaster; he was waved through the turnstiles with an admonition to get himself clean before making his report.

Like a latter-day Ishmael, Greg stood looking over the waters towards Peterborough which, like almost all cities, clung around the stones of the dead religion. He remained, sack over his shoulder until the stink of his pelts, fouled from the pits, urged him to turn for the station.

All was orderly there.

Peter let him through the side gate. The guard kept a wry-faced distance from the pungent cartographer saying: "De-con's all ready for you Greg, water is 41°C, and waiting, with baited breath…".

The taint of odour was a near-tangible representation of just how close to the precipice of chaos humanity stood, Greg knew, they all knew. Seventy years of creeping tides and rapid isolation had left a scar in the minds of the Highlanders. But for knowledge, they too would be reduced to incest and cannibalism.

Called simply 'bipeds' by the citizenry, the insular survivors who dwelt in their own ordure were evidence incarnate of the truth of The Tenets: Opportunity, Understanding and Choice; that this alone kept humanity from slipping into endless dark ages.

***

Lydia stood beyond the glazed de-con chamber, picking greengages in the warm October breeze. The gentle glow of stored light enhanced by the mirror complex all but banished the dark. She greeted Greg with a mildness which flagged itself as a warning: "Good evening, Cartographer, what fresh horrors have you to soothe me with tonight?"

"Nothing you've not lost sleep over before. Ella is approximately six months into her pregnancy, and as healthy as can be expected for someone who's not seen the sun since she began to show." Greg laid the contents of his sack on a steel tray and stripped off as he talked. Placing the sack together with his clothes into the steamer, he stepped into the inner chamber; where he systematically scrubbed every inch of his body with astringent soap.

"Will she carry to term?" Lydia paused in her harvest to look the steaming, naked man over. Greg's answer came without hesitation: "Unlikely, Missus said Ella came out after just three months, but they count pregnancy from the time they notice swelling. As the fourth generation of first degree consanguineal parentage, I expect homozygosity to render the foetus infertile. I have the usual samples to assess degradation in the adults."

Lydia snorted, pushing out her words: "Adult? Malnutrition aside, the female Ella resembles a ten-year old. I accept from her pregnancy that she's passed adolescence… Cartographer, I believe prolonged contact with the bipeds is affecting your judgement." She stood head-cocked, watching him towel himself dry and step into a paper one-piece. "We will convene together with Assessment One at 0900 tomorrow. Have your report in place for review."

Greg watched the Director's form recede into the unit, his weariness lost in the understanding that his night would be long in preparation for the morrow. This review would give the Director and Assessors an opportunity to eradicate the scraps of humanity he had brought to their attention. Choice was the only protection against murder.

***

Narrow windows leant bright stripes across whitewashed walls; the rich ochre of the tiled floor, the streamlined oak tables—each scrubbed to a bleached gold. Greg had been readying himself in the briefing room two hours before Assessment One entered, themselves half-an-hour early.

With muted greetings they settled around the room. The soft greens of the assessor's uniforms and the tan of Greg's own mellowed to a coming fall.

Their murmurs fell softly into the space. In quiet order files were placed on tables; espadrille-shod feet padded gently as the de-facto court readied for debate. Argument and fact twirled in Greg's mind, fear of today's outcome acknowledged, slowing his movements. He now had no doubt that today would determine when a cleansing would be instigated in the Eastern flats, as it had in the South. One-hundred and thirty-seven bipeds cleansed from the Westminster archipelago.

Lydia's tread was heard in the corridor, and the future began.

"Assessors Phyllis and Grant, Cartographer Greg, we convene on this day, the thirtieth of October 2023 at 0900, to discuss the implications of allowing the bipeds of the Eastern flats continued residence within our patronage." Pausing to allow her stenographer to signal readiness, Greg took the opportunity to speak: "Director Lydia, thank you for arranging this assessment. May I request a clarification of terms?"

Lydia nodded, eyes narrowing. "Thank you, Director." Greg continued: "By "the bipeds of the Eastern flats", you refer to the human settlements ringed by the highlands of Wisbech, Ely, Bury, Diss and Norwich? And that by "continued residence" you mean continued life?" Lydia gazed at the young man. Pausing, she responded in clear tones: "Yes, and yes, Cartographer. Our judgement is all we have, our morals and educated interpretation of circumstance. The definitions of humanity do not apply to these bipeds. They have no understanding, no desire for it."

"Empirically, Director, these are humans – your opinion may be that they are degraded and through lack of opportunity have been forced to, take what is available. Director, Assessors, they are children without experience. We do not kill our children because they are ignorant, we educate them."

"Your compassion does you credit, Cartographer. But these bipeds are not children—as you are determined to class the female Ella as an adult, please, do not argue—they pose the threats of disease and violence to us and each other. Have they poisoned your mind that you can't understand?"

"I understand these examples of what HUMANITY might be as essential to our development—Director, I bow to your experience with regards to the horrors of The Tumult. I believe these exemplars of what happens when people become distanced from civilisation are surely essential to our own adherence to…"

"They, Cartographer, chose not to be civilised. CHOICE itself is the key tenet of humanity! The beasts of The Tumult were the sort who, like your pit dwellers, opted to remain in filth, rutting, feasting on whatever was to hand."

"Following The Tumult, we of The Great Highlands too were considered subhuman. Director Lydia, may I remind you that had not The Great Cull been halted by The Reckoning, I would have never drawn breath, and you too would have been extinguished—cleansed—by the American Pastoral Army. All I say is that these people, these bipeds, be given opportunity to live out their lives which will come to a short end of their own accord."

The assessors looked at each other in silent agreement. Assessor Grant spoke: "Assessment One, comprising Assessors Phyllis and Grant: 70213431, confirm with gratitude that the patronage of Director Lydia is continued, upon her agreement to be submitted within one week, for the next three cycles. We announce that Cartographer Greg is requested to henceforth accept the burden of Advisor to Director Lydia for a single cycle."

"We are convinced and comforted that your sufferings will ensure the balance required for existential harmony in this bastion of civilisation. Your investitures will be solemnised upon your return to Peterborough. With regard to the bipeds, we are assured that whichever course you settle upon will be the correct one, at this time and in this place. Opportunity, Understanding and Choice. You embody these tenets. Your judgements are final."

The assessors rose and left.

The warm strips of sunlight moved two inches across the walls before Greg spoke; "Director Lydia, have I been burdened with authority and power?"

Lydia considered before replying; "Assessor, this is indeed a burden, which must be how power works. I have declined the burden before, and watched, impotent, as improper judgements were enacted. I have had no advisor in two cycles. I accept the possibility that I may be the one become tainted, and that you will be, perhaps, my purgative."

Silence lingered before Lydia spoke, "Greg, I add my request, Advisor."

Greg allowed his Understanding to encompass the change. He acknowledged the Opportunity. He Chose to accept it.

Gently, he sang: "rompin stompin yompin frooh tha trees, no skin on ands nd nun un nees, scrubble froo tha rubble roost meat fur tea."

Our Authors —

Jordan Aitcheson is a first year English Literature and Creative Writing Student. He finds the process of writing poetry cathartic and uses a lot of his poems as tools to understand himself and the world around him. One of his main influences is Hip-Hop because of its ethos of self-expression and he says he looks up to a lot of artists from this genre for inspiration e.g. Kendrick Lamar. As he continues to grow, he hopes his writing will as well so he can stretch himself to explore more forms and styles

Joe Bird is originally from Kent and is currently reading American Literature and Creative Writing at an Undergraduate level at UEA. Having always taken a lot of inspiration from film and music as well as the work of other authors, reading his work is a very vivid visual experience, merging a sensory environment with surreal and dream-like monologues.

Thai Braddick is a queer, non-binary poet and activist studying American Literature with Creative Writing. They believe in hope-filled anarchy, kissing friends, and community care. They want to teach English and maybe be part of a revolution some day.

Leia Butler is a second-year English Literature and Creative Writing student. She loves writing experimental poetry and trying to find new ways to present ideas on the page. She a previous winner of the Streetcake experimental writing prize. Leia channels her love for writing through editing Arts for Concrete and being Vice-President for Creative Writing Society. Originally from London, Leia loves the writing scene there but has fallen even deeper in love with writing in Norwich due to its beautiful scenery.

Daisy Campbell is a first-year undergraduate student studying English Literature with Creative Writing. She is interested in poetry which explores the possibilities of cross-disciplinary arts collaborations, especially those which take place on the illustrated page.

Charlotte Cassidy is a Second Year LDC student studying English Literature with Creative Writing at the University of East Anglia. Although she is mainly a prose writer, she also enjoys attending open mics to perform her poetry along with writing for the stage. Her work often romanticises aspects of everyday life whilst dealing with contemporary culture. She uses metaphorical and symbolic language to produce imagery within her creative pieces, giving her writing a vivid style that is tied to the emotional journey of her characters.

Andrew Constantinou was born and raised in Nicosia, Cyprus. Having also lived in Tripoli, Libya as well as Glasgow, Scotland and most recently Norwich, England, Constantinou possesses the unique perspective of a "citizen of the world", a viewpoint which becomes apparent in his piece.

Dylan Davies, born in Derby, is a second year English Literature and Creative Writing student at UEA. They once said that they would never write poetry, but now, after being published in art collectives such as !GWAK and 'I Don't Want to Go Insane' zine, they seem to have changed their mind. This is their second year in the UEA Undergraduate Anthology.

Sasha Donovan-Anns is currently in her first year reading English Literature and Creative Writing (BA) at UEA. Drawing from her experiences with chronic illness, she usually writes pieces that engage with health—both physical and mental. Predominantly a poet, she also seeks to interweave her own queer identity through romantic pieces, creating a little more of the representation she wished to see as a young adult. She is determined to bring an uplifting quality to her confessional style.

Helen Drumm studies American Literature and Creative Writing at UEA. She is from Middlesbrough and is half French. She did a year abroad in California, and can confirm that it is merely a state of mind. She's the 'It' girl of the Norwich celestial synth-punk poetry scene. She has written a zine called Hairy Girls about being very hairy.

Isabel Edain studies English Literature and Creative Writing at UEA. They aspire to be a fop but alas—being poor, they are only a poet. Their writing deals with dreams, rodents, changelings, and weird decaying cities that they made up. In a past life they were a winter stoat.

Ally Fowler is an English Literature with Creative Writing student, specialising in the magical and the mythical. She cites Max Porter, Jeanette Winterson, and Natasha Pulley as inspirations, and her greatest achievement is reading the entirety of 'Les Miserables' without giving up or crying.

Chloe Gainford is at 3rd Year American Literature with Creative Writing student and self-proclaimed northern powerhouse, her work particularly focuses around the dramatic narrative, as set in prose, and the construction of the mind. When she is not nose-deep in a book, you can find her working every hour under the sun in retail or organising trips (both within and outside the UK, before the descent on the coronavirus of course) for UEA Korfball. She will soon be trading in novels for keys and a baton as she undertakes life as a Prison Guard upon graduating. Sebastian Gale is a second year English Literature and Creative Writing student.

Sebastian Gale is a second year English Literature and Creative Writing student.

Emma Goodyear is a final year American Literature with Creative Writing student. Originally a prose and script writer, her degree inspired her to face her fear of poetry, which she now thinks is the vastly superior medium. In spite of this, her biggest writing goal is to finish the fantasy thriller novel she dreamed up when she was fifteen. She spends most of her time drinking hot chocolate, procrastinating on The Sims, and 'borrowing' her friend's cat for cuddles. Her poems 'Longing' and 'notes to a younger self' mark her first appearance in one of UEA's Creative Writing Anthologies

Sam Gordon-Webb is a student studying English Literature with Creative Writing. His poetry has published for Ulalume Lighthouse, and he regularly performs his work at open mics and poetry recitals in the city of Norwich. Having recovered from an eating disorder, Sam also writes about issues pertaining to mental health awareness and writes a regular column in Concrete dedicated to such matters. Sam grew up in Washington D.C but now lives in London with loving parents, two sisters, and a lazy but equally lovable labrador, Toffee.

The being currently holding the name of **Alex Grenfell** is a writer from Oxfordshire, although originally sired on the planet Kolob in the vicinity of Qzz'tar. After reigning as a bloodthirsty despot for centuries on Kolob, a rebellion occurring on the 12thof November 1999 in human decades forced him into the prison of flesh he currently occupies. The only escape, he finds, is writing angry poetry directed to the current reigning governments of Earth. He also enjoys long walks on the beach.

Oliver Hancock is a second year English Literature and Creative Writing student. Originally from Cambridge, he came to UEA in order to develop his skills as a poet. As a result, he has been published multiple times in the art collective !GWAK and plans to continue performing at UEA Live. This is his first year in the UEA Undergraduate Anthology.

Ida Bang Hansen, born 1997, grew up in Aarhus in Denmark. Before she knew how to spell, she wrote and illustrated several small books. Her incredible creativity showed in the fact that the recurring main character was a girl by the name 'girl'. Ida now studies for a degree in Cognitive Science and is spending the final semester abroad in Norwich (where she luckily managed to sneak in a module on creative writing). The course has given her insights about the human mind and behaviour, which she uses to bring life to her characters on the page.

Kasper Hassett was born in London and is a second year student at the University of East Anglia, studying English Literature with Creative Writing. He writes primarily prose and some poetry, informed by his experiences of being both queer and working-class. In fiction, he is interested in portraying how aspects of background, such as housing and education, affect lives, and to what extent individuals

can determine their fate. 'Keeping Company' explores loneliness in the LGBTQ+ community.

Maddi Hastings currently spends her time between writing poetry and prose, unsure on what form she likes best. Currently, she is in her second year studying English Literature with Creative Writing at UEA, taking a particular interest in creating work which adopts a slightly, surreal, introspective and otherwise warped, view of the world, its people, and their experiences, both intimate and personal, and recognisable and universal.

Siobhan Horner-Galvin is completely confused. Born in Libya to Irish and Indian parents, the question she loathes is, 'Where are you from?' She lives in an old, Dutch barge on the river Deben and seems to be on the continual hunt for something: the perfect masala dosa, a draught Guinness or the feeling of 'home'. Going into her final year of English Literature and Creative Writing, her writing is often concerned with secrets; anyone who claims to have no secrets is immediately under suspicion. This theme reoccurs in her writing, as does concern with more marginalised characters.

Charlie Humphreys was born in 1996, and that's when the problems started. His formative years were spent in Cambridge where, encouraged by his English teacher, he decided he would pursue a career in writing. He's currently finishing a degree in English Literature and Creative Writing. It seems to be going alright so far. All the stories he tells are true, except the ones that aren't.

Ben'J Jordan grew up in North West London before moving to Norwich to study English Literature and

Creative Writing at UEA. His debut novel is currently being penned.

Erin Ketteridge is a second year English Literature with Creative Writing student, born and raised in Norfolk. Despite the lack of contact with the outside world that growing up in such a county means, she still learned to read and write almost as well as her UEA peers. Erin dreams of one day living in a cottage on the coast with many dogs, and having an illustrious career as a writer to fund her wild lifestyle. She enjoys drinking tea, long walks on the beach, and being published in Undergraduate Anthologies. She plans on studying for a Masters after graduation.

Sebastian Lloyd is a first year UEA English Literature and Creative writing student from South East London. He has been performing spoken word since he was 17 at nights such as Poetry cafe and SET Dalston.

Chris Matthews is a third year English literature and creative writing student. He predominantly writes natural lyrical poetry and has recently been exploring physicality and grief with his writing.

Zoe Mitchell is a first-year undergraduate at UEA. Aside from the obvious – reading and writing – she loves singing, planning movie nights and eating far too much pizza. She has been a writer for as long as she can remember: even before she could hold a pen, she told stories to anyone who would listen (however unwillingly). When not at UEA, Zoe lives near Dundee in Scotland. She enjoys the culture – but not the weather!

Arcadia Molinas Argimon is a writer. She was born in Madrid and has lived all her life between Spain and the UK with one rouge year in Colorado, USA. Arcadia's style is best described as having an erotic investment in portentous existential questions.

Farah Mostafa is a third year English Literature with Creative Writing student. She is a proud Luxembourgish-Egyptian who is insanely passionate about human rights and social justice, to the point of her friends ignoring her when she goes on about the racist implications of old Disney movies. She loves spending her time watching too much TV, and boasts about knowing the entire soundtrack to Hamilton, even though she really shouldn't. Her flatmates know her as the puppy of the house, because she is often the most excitable and childish one around, despite being the oldest one

Chiara Picchi is a third year Literature and History student originally from Italy and Luxembourg. She focuses primarily on flash fiction and short stories and whilst darker themes often feature in her work, she also enjoys exploring all things aesthetic and the mundanity of everyday life. The role of imagery and sound is also a key point of interest for her and often plays an important role in her pieces.

Jack Pletts' writing takes inspiration from his feelings regarding the relocation of Francis Bacon's Imaginary Portrait of Pope Pius XII from its own display wall near the main entrance of the Sainsbury Centre for Visual Arts to a shared wall in its remote northern corner. This has made it difficult for Pletts to leave his bed in the morning and find enjoyment in life.

Jeanie Purslow is a 21-year-old South Londoner, singer/songwriter and poet in her third year of studying English Literature with Creative Writing. After her degree she wants to do nothing in Norwich but work a rubbish job and play at every open mic night in town. She doesn't know much yet, but she does know that she adores all animals and writing about herself in the third person has never gone marvellously for her.

Rose Ramsden would like to write a funny bio but, ultimately, is not witty enough to do so. Instead, she will talk about her poetry that has been previously published by Venue, The Punch Magazine, !GWAK, and others. This makes her sound professional and accomplished. She assures you, she is not.

Cormac Rea is a final year student, currently undertaking a BA in American Literature with Creative Writing. Having grown up on the Irish border, much of Cormac's work is deeply indebted both topically and stylistically to the region. He explores many of the issues that have historically affected his homeland both socially and psychologically: identity, division, and trauma are all pervasive throughout. He seeks to portray the effects of this legacy, whether subtle or profound, on the youth and young adulthood of the 'ceasefire baby' generation, growing up in a scarred place with its own considerable growing pains to nurse

Julia Reynolds is a first year English Literature and Creative Writing student whose hobbies include trying her best to write things she doesn't hate and drinking too much tea.

Saskia Reynolds is a second-year English Literature with Creative Writing student who, on occasion, fancies herself a misplaced woodland nymph. Her writing is preoccupied with interrogating the extremes of the human experience. She is particularly inspired by the works of Murakami and Scandi-noir fiction.

Tom Rosser was raised in Elmbridge and is currently a second-year Creative Writing and English Literature BA student at UEA. Prior to this, he worked for several years as a Barista in Central London and much of his current writing draws from his observations, experiences and reflections of that time. He is the recipient of no literary scholarships and his works have garnered zero critical praise.

Leo Schrey-Yeats is a first year on the English Literature with Creative Writing course, where aspiring writers go to be shouted at until they come out good. It's usually very constructive and supportive shouting. When not reciting lines from The Hitchhiker's Guide to the Galaxy, Leo is usually looking for more wacky inspiration to make his plotlines needlessly messy, which will ultimately result in him agonising over them at a later date. That's life he supposes.

Oliver Shrouder is a first-year English Literature with Creative Writing student from UEA. Hailing from Grantham, twice voted the most boring town in England, Oliver was inspired to write anything he could to escape from it. Now a poet, he explores wildlife in the hope that the Norwich air can blow Grantham's smog from his hair.

Toby Skinner is in the first year of his English Literature with Creative Writing degree. His work has also appeared in the creative writing section of UEA's student newspaper Concrete, along with his recent ghost story, The Left Crematorium, being featured on the newspapers website. As well as creative writing, Toby enjoys surfing, reading ghost fiction and finding great t-shirts in charity shops.

Lily Stirling is a third year studying English Literature with Creative Writing. She grew up in rural Suffolk and has a special place in her heart for the East Anglian countryside. In her short stories and prose, she has often drawn on nature and the wonders of the landscapes surrounding her. However, since starting UEA, Lily's writing style has transformed into an often distinct narrative with a dark story line. She has enjoyed developing voices usually through misfit characters that she has produced whilst studying at UEA. She is currently working on an anthology of her own short stories.

Madu Udeh writes poems in dialogue with the internet. Trending words and #'s, rapper type beats and lo-fi, untold histories and internet archives - Madu translates a visual mesh through text and frequently places his own visuals next to found footage to aid in the storytelling process.

Meg Watts would describe herself as a full-time environmentalist with a part-time student gig, although she is supposed to be studying her first year of BA Literature and Creative Writing. She has been publishing her poetry, prose, art, photography and filmmaking on her blogs since age sixteen, but now writes for Concrete Student Newspaper, Forget The Youth, The Hourglass, !Gwak Mag and various online outlets. Meg is currently working on her own environmental magazine, At Home, On Earth, alongside juggling her graphics work for Global Climate Justice and rapidly growing Oulipo poetry collection.

Yap Shi Quan is an English undergraduate from Nanyang Technological University, and has had the privilege of having a student exchange in University of East Anglia, School of Literature, Drama and Creative Writing for a semester. He enjoys all kinds of stories, be it in the form of books, movies, video games, and anime/manga. Just don't call him an otaku—he will violently reject that label. He blames his parents and grandmother for not teaching him Cantonese and Hokkien, although, frankly, it's his own fault for not proactively learning it.

Katherine Yong Yhap is in the third year of her English Literature and Creative Writing BA at UEA. Now in her fourth decade, she hopes her future will be as mixed as her past. Katherine claims heritage of her Guyanese, Italian, Chinese, German, Mongolian, Jewish and Amerindian forebears; and her job titles have included housewife and glazier. She has called many cities home; but feels now that Norwich will never be out from under her skin. Within the arts, her inclusion within this anthology is the pinnacle of her achievement thus far; and she intends to be back for more.

Eggbox Publishing Committee —

President
Martha Griffiths

Vice President
Emma Seager

Secretary & Union Council Rep
Oliver Shrouder

Treasurer & Workshop Coordinator
Farah Mostafa

Health & Safety Officer
Hannah Graham

Equality & Diversity Officer
Dylan Davies

First Year Rep & Social Media Officer
Daisy Church

With Thanks To —

Editor-in-Chief
Martha Griffiths

Editors
Abigail Braim
Arcadia Molinas Argimon
Ben'J Jordan
Chloe Utting
Daisy Church
Dylan Davies
Elle Guyan
Flo Pearce-Higginson
Georgia Greetham
Hannah Graham
Jack Oxford
Julia Reynolds
Katherine Cadregari
Maya Coomarasamy
Nerisse Appleby
Olivia McCourry
Ryan Lenney
Saskia Reynolds

Marketing and Sales
Anna Mitkova
Daisy Church
Elle Guyan
Emma Goodyear
Farah Mostafa
Hannah Lee
Jack Oxford
Julia Reynolds
Madu U
Sophie Wallwin

UNDERSCORE

First published by Egg Box Publishing 2020
Part of UEA Publishing Project Ltd
International ©2020 retained by individual authors
A CIO record of this book is available
from the British Library

This book is sold subject to the condition that it
shall not, by way of trade or otherwise, be lent,
resold, hired out, stored in retrieval system, or
otherwise circulated without the publisher's prior
consent in any form of binding or cover other
than that in which it is published and without
a similar condition including the condition
being imposed on the subsequent purchaser.

Underscore is typeset in Adobe Garamond Pro
Designed and typeset by Anna Brewster
Printed and bound in the UK by Imprint Digital
Distributed by NBN International

ISBN: 978-1911343936

U